Praise for *Conscious C*

D0446221

"Conscious Communications *is a real*i*s...., p*r*actical, and extremely powerful guide for turning your life into a joyful ride no matter how troubled it may be today. I will be keeping it by my bedside and referring to it often. You will want to as well."*

— **Sonia Choquette,** *New York Times* best-selling author of *Your 3 Best Super Powers*

"Conscious Communications *positively changes your association to the words you use for yourself and others."*

— **Mike Dooley,** *New York Times* best-selling author of *From Deep Space with Love*

"Anyone who feels the itch to dig in and completely transform their own lives and create a glorious new reality will benefit powerfully from Mary Shores's new book, Conscious Communications. *Mary provides acres of support and insight as she teaches us to journal our way to living power- fully and changing our destiny. Mary went from an unthinkable tragedy to a victorious and glorious life, and teaches us all to do the same."*

— **Regena Thomashauer,** *New York Times* best-selling author of *Pussy*

"Mary Shores shares the treasure chest of transformative tools and lessons she learned along her own healing journey out of the darkness and into the light. Conscious Communications *is a compelling compendium of stories, processes, and exercises creating a compass that leads right to the heart of what you can do to activate your greatest potential."*

— **Nancy Levin,** author of *Worthy*

CONSCIOUS
COMMUNICATIONS

Hay House Titles of Related Interest

YOU CAN HEAL YOUR LIFE, the movie,
starring Louise Hay & Friends
(available as a 1-DVD program, an expanded 2-DVD set, and as an
online streaming video)
Learn more at www.hayhouse.com/louise-movie

THE SHIFT, the movie,
starring Dr. Wayne W. Dyer
(available as a 1-DVD program, an expanded 2-DVD set, and as an
online streaming video)
Learn more at www.hayhouse.com/the-shift-movie

❧

E-SQUARED: Nine Do-It-Yourself Energy Experiments
That Prove Your Thoughts Create Your Reality, by Pam Grout

LIFE LOVES YOU: 7 Spiritual Practices to Heal Your Life,
by Louise Hay and Robert Holden

THE MOTIVATION MANIFESTO: 9 Declarations to
Claim Your Personal Power, by Brendon Burchard

THE UNIVERSE HAS YOUR BACK: Transform Fear to Faith,
by Gabrielle Bernstein

YOU ARE THE PLACEBO: Making Your Mind Matter,
by Dr. Joe Dispenza

All of the above are available at your local bookstore,
or may be ordered by visiting:

Hay House USA: www.hayhouse.com®
Hay House Australia: www.hayhouse.com.au
Hay House UK: www.hayhouse.co.uk
Hay House South Africa: www.hayhouse.co.za
Hay House India: www.hayhouse.co.in

CONSCIOUS
COMMUNICATIONS

**YOUR STEP=BY=STEP GUIDE
TO HARNESSING THE POWER
OF YOUR WORDS**
TO CHANGE YOUR MIND,
YOUR CHOICES,
AND YOUR LIFE

MARY SHORES

HAY HOUSE, INC.
Carlsbad, California • New York City
London • Sydney • Johannesburg
Vancouver • New Delhi

Published and distributed in the United States by: Hay House, Inc.: www .hayhouse.com® • *Published and distributed in Australia by:* Hay House Australia Pty. Ltd.: www.hayhouse.com.au • *Published and distributed in the United Kingdom by:* Hay House UK, Ltd.: www.hayhouse.co.uk • *Published and distributed in the Republic of South Africa by:* Hay House SA (Pty), Ltd.: www.hayhouse.co.za • *Distributed in Canada by:* Raincoast Books: www.raincoast.com • *Published in India by:* Hay House Publishers India: www.hayhouse.co.in

Cover design: Karla Baker • *Interior design:* Nick C. Welch

Cataloging-in-Publication Data is on file at the Library of Congress

Tradepaper ISBN: 978-1-4019-5213-6

10 9 8 7 6 5 4 3 2
1st edition, August 2017

Printed in the United States of America

SUSTAINABLE FORESTRY INITIATIVE

Certified Sourcing
www.sfiprogram.org
SFI-01268

SFI label applies to text stock only

This is for my two sons, my friends, and dedicated team who have always given me unconditional love and support.

CONTENTS

WHY YOU NEED TO USE CONSCIOUS COMMUNICATIONS:
AN INTRODUCTION

WHERE IT STARTED

Whatever made you pick up this book—whether it was the cover, a friend's advice, having nothing to read at the airport—there was a reason. Maybe you're finding it difficult to get up in the morning lately. Maybe you have goals but you don't know how to create a life that is in alignment with those goals. Perhaps you feel—you *know*—that you have a bigger purpose in life but you don't know what it is. Or you might just be trying to figure out why you can't seem to feel optimistic anymore. Whatever the reason was, you're here now. You're ready to take steps to change all that.

I've been where you are, and I have gathered tools, advice, and exercises that have not only pushed me through my darkest days but have also propelled me forward so that I am living a life that is better than I ever dreamed it could be. Let me help you understand the thoughts, words, and actions that are holding you back and bring those thoughts, words, and actions into alignment with your dreams. I'll share with you my own experiences, some background on the way the brain works, and small, actionable steps that will help you move forward with such ease that you won't even realize how quickly your life is improving.

This is not a book full of empty promises. I'm not going to tell you that you're going to be rich or that you will meet the love of your life after doing the exercises, but I can promise that if you read and complete this book, you will move in the direction you want to be traveling and you will be closer to your dreams than ever before. You may create new dreams along the way, or take steps toward goals you once felt were impossible.

A lot of these exercises will involve journaling. I truly believe the intimacy of writing to yourself is the best way to really examine your own thoughts and actions. Go ahead and pick out a notebook—something beautiful that inspires you to write. Keep a pen and highlighter handy so that you can make notes and emphasize the sections that you want to remember. This journal is only for you, so please let yourself be honest while engaging in the exercises. You have nothing to lose and everything to gain.

By reading this book, you are committing to creating a better version of yourself. You have the resolve to take the necessary steps toward creating goals and achieving them. Let's get started!

HI, I'M MARY SHORES

So what makes me qualified to write this life-changing self-empowerment book?

After a rough childhood, the devastating death of my first child, the creation of my own successful and unique collection agency, an unexpected and messy divorce, raising an autistic son, and the ups and downs of over 40 years of life, I discovered that I had an immense well of resilience. I had developed tools that could help others empower themselves to create the life they had always imagined. My greatest dream was for Hay House to publish my book, but there was a hitch—I kept saying to myself, *I want to write a book, but I'm not a writer.*

Inside our mind, we all have this little committee that is constantly criticizing us, and each time we allow that committee to take control, we are actually making it stronger, reinforcing the neural pathways created by the belief system that gave us those thoughts in the first place.

I used to say things like *Everything is a struggle* and *I'm such a mess*. I would get very descriptive about it, saying that I felt as if every day I was trying to walk down a set of stairs and someone was kicking them out from underneath me. I didn't just *say* that I felt like a mess; I had to *illustrate* it and really articulate all the ways I was struggling and messy. Does this sound familiar? Do you find yourself making statements like *I'll never be able to afford that*, or *He's so lucky*? I think we all do. But eventually I realized this was only bringing more mess and struggle to my life.

What I had to do was be deliberate about the things coming out of my mouth. I would stop myself from complaining midsentence. I started saying instead, *My life is easy and effortless*. Sometimes it would be too hard for me to actually *say* the words, so I would write them down instead. *My life is easy and effortless. My life is easy. I have a life of joy.* The more I did this, the more I started making decisions that would make that true, decisions in direct alignment with what I wanted.

Those words worked. Words are incredibly powerful, and the right words work in my personal life, and they work in my business.

I am the CEO of a collection agency. Not really what you think of when you use the words *enlightened* or *happiness*, right? Me either—at first. The shift began after I went to a Tony Robbins event in 2005, when I got my first foot in the door of the personal development world and it changed everything for me. I came away from that conference with two basic but life-changing ideas: what you focus on grows, and always know your outcome. I went back to my office and thought about that. What did I want my outcome to be? I realized that I didn't want my outcome to be *make a ton of money* or *be a hotshot*. All I wanted was the next person I spoke with on the phone to be happier at the end of the call than they were at the start.

That one choice changed my entire life. Ten years later I'd developed an entire system I call Conscious Communications, a

customer-service program that changed the way we do business
—and made us much more successful.

Conscious Communications is a simple process that consists
of eliminating negative language, using words that work, and
focusing on what you want.

We start with a very basic principle: *stop saying negative words*.
We have a Do Not Say list that includes words like *no, not*, and
can't. We replace them with words like *I'm happy to check into
that for you* or *I want to assure you that we're going to be able to help
you with this*, and we always say what we *can* do instead of what
we can't.

You may be thinking that this sounds impractical for your
day-to-day life, but I'm here to tell you that changing your words
has the ability to change your life, and I will show you how.

DO NOT SAY LIST	
1. No	4. Won't
2. Not	5. However
3. Can't	6. Unfortunately

SO WHAT'S THAT GOT TO DO WITH YOU!

This book—and this process—is about creating reality. The
words we use when we talk to ourselves and to others have
an enormous impact on our life. We manifest our own reality
through what we speak about, what we think about, what our
belief systems are, and how we feel. This has to do with the way
our brain evolved and the way we use our mind. If that's got

you scratching your head, don't worry. The first part of the book explains exactly how this works, and once you understand your brain, you can learn to take control of it.

In their research, many neuroscientists have determined that most of our thoughts on any given day are the exact same as the day before. That's why, if you want to change your reality, you need to change your thoughts with purpose. If you focus on something new, something better, your life can change. Just like when I focused on *I want the next person who calls to be happier at the end of the call*—that thought changed my entire world.

Of course, there is more to it than just thought. Our conscious mind is very powerful, but our subconscious is no slouch—and is harder to control. Our subconscious creates and maintains our belief systems through synapses and neural pathways that get more and more ingrained over time. What we believe controls much of what we create in our life, and so many of us are held back by our limiting beliefs. I think of them as barrier beliefs, because if you have a negative belief system, it doesn't just limit you, it actually puts a wall between you and your dreams. Remember, I had that dream to write a book but I kept telling myself that I wasn't a writer. So it didn't matter how hard I focused on that dream—as long as I had that barrier belief, there was no way for me to get over that wall. I had to learn how to break through that barrier first.

The next piece of the puzzle is the nervous system, which controls our emotions and our feelings. I'm a huge fan of Bruce Lipton, Ph.D., best-selling author of *The Honeymoon Effect* and several other books. He's a brilliant cellular biologist, and he understands the chemistry of the body at a cellular level. Have you ever heard the phrases *We have something affecting us on a cellular level* or *The issues are in the tissues*? These are referring to how the nervous system stores our past traumas. And it tends to be reactive: if some kind of emergency happens to us, our nervous system can put us into fight-or-flight mode, sending signals throughout the body to create a specific chemical recipe. A "state of emergency" chemical recipe is a cocktail of adrenaline, cortisone, aldosterone, and other hormones, all of which are designed to make us react quickly. If we're falling in love, we have the honeymoon chemical recipe—oxytocin, dopamine, and vasopressin. We feel a genuine chemical high when we're falling in love.

This is all well and good when it's working properly, but problems can occur when an event triggers a memory in our nervous system. These are the obstacles we've got to overcome to create our ideal life.

THIS TOO SHALL PASS

Next we will get into the idea of probabilities. We all have unlimited probabilities—anything at all could happen. It's the choices we make from moment to moment that determine our future, leading us to a variety of magical adventures.

So how do you make sure you're making the right choices—choices that will increase the probability that you will lead the life you want?

Let's start with something most of us struggle with at one time or another—our finances. To me, money is energy. It's an exchange. How you take in that energy and how you give it out really determines your financial outcome. Throughout my life I have always felt as though I was the richest person in the world. I remember, in the early stages of my business, that the first few times I got a paycheck (which was only a couple hundred bucks at best), I was so proud. I remember taking that check to the bank and thinking to myself, *These tellers must be so impressed when they see the amount on this check.* They probably couldn't have cared less, but—and this probably seems ridiculous—I really believed it. *I felt abundant.* And that abundance has grown with my confidence in my abilities.

The only financial, physical, and mental diet I have ever followed was the idea of "cleanse or clog." All I do is I look at a piece of food and say, *Will this cleanse me or clog me?* And if it's going to clog me, I use the 80/20 rule. Eighty percent of the time, I eat something cleansing, and then 20 percent of the time, I can have that piece of chocolate or cake or coffee or whatever it is that I choose.

"Cleanse or clog" works in all areas of life. Think about removing or repositioning every choice or behavior that does not serve your core desire. Remember when I used to say my life was a mess? Well, it *was* a mess, because I was saying I wanted one thing but my choices and behaviors and beliefs were leading me in another direction. Chaos! When you hear thought leaders say you need to be "in alignment," this is what they are referring to.

When I used to hear that phrase, I would think, *What the heck does that mean?* It took me a long time to understand this idea of alignment, and how we spend much of our life out of alignment because we are making choices that are not authentic, that aren't a match with what we really desire. Beautiful things can happen when we detach ourselves from all those things that are not going to get us closer to what we really want.

SO HOW DO I DO THAT?

Thoughts are beautiful things, and so are words. The heart of Conscious Communications is the idea that you can create your own reality—and you can do so using words and thoughts. The five types of expressions are self-talk, spoken words, affirmations, goals, and gratitude.

Self-talk. Self-talk exists in the conscious mind, and it passes through as instructions to the subconscious mind. Our subconscious mind doesn't know what is "bad" or "good," it only knows what we tell it. This is why I often compare it to a computer, in the way it runs programs based on our commands. What we say to ourselves are "instructions," and these are brought into reality by our subconscious mind. This is how self-talk creates our reality.

Spoken words. What you talk about is a mirror of what is inside your mind. In order to immerse yourself in the life you want to create, you must use deliberately aligned speech. Whether you realize it or not, the words you speak are what you are affirming for your life. The words you use, whether they are your thoughts or are spoken aloud, have a big impact on you. Create the reality you want in spoken words, bringing them to life outside of your mind.

Affirmations. Affirmations are declarations. You assert that what you want to be true *is* true. Through the creation and repetition of words or phrases, affirmations become a tool to reprogram your mind. We all have a daily practice of repeating affirmations and mantras, even if we don't realize it. We have built this daily practice over time, and the more often we choose a word or phrase to focus on, the more natural the practice becomes for us. In time these new words and phrases will change who we are.

Goals. There's plenty of scientific research out there that says that the difference between people who achieve success in life and those who do not is that the achievers regularly write goals for themselves and follow a plan to make the goals happen. Written goals demonstrate the desire to achieve something; they are a tool to create a specific intention that connects to a desired achievement.

Gratitude. Gratitude can be a feeling (emotion) and/or an attitude (mind-set). It's what we use to acknowledge a benefit that we have received or will receive. Gratitude is a fundamental quality within us all—every language in the world has a way of saying *thank you*. Gratitude as an attitude or mind-set implies that we have voluntarily made a choice to focus on the good we have. Gratitude puts situations into perspective. Remember that we create our own reality, and when we focus on looking for the good, it becomes easier for us to spot that good with less effort. By practicing awareness of the positive things in life, we fight off the brain's natural tendency to scan for, and spot, the negatives. As a result we train our brain to be more positive and see more possibilities—enabling us to make more positive choices.

Remember that for years and years the thoughts you've had have circulated throughout your brain, creating neural networks, making those patterns your natural default. The person you are today was conditioned by this repetition. By making your affirmations real and personal, you will make different choices and align yourself with your desires. Practicing affirmations daily will reprogram your brain, creating new neural pathways, a new perspective, a host of new ideas, and a path to experiences that will make your affirmations your new default. Keep going! Every day brings you closer to what it is that you truly desire.

When you've got the three pillars of transforming your life—focus, beliefs, and chemistry—in alignment, you'll be able to make aligned choices, which will change the probabilities of the outcomes in your life.

At the end of the book, you will create a one-page action plan. I always think with the end result in mind, so start with a goal or something that you want. Next ask yourself, *What are five or six things that have to be true in order for this goal to be reached?* From there you will take each one of those bullets and write out two or three action items that will be the steps to be taken to get you closer and closer to your end result. When you are finished, you will have a one-page action plan, and you will know everything you have to do to get to where you want to be.

IS IT REALLY THAT SIMPLE?

Simple? Yes. Easy? Well, that depends on you. Sometimes your barrier beliefs are very obvious, and in that case you can take action to create new neural pathways. Give yourself some affirmations, and *boom!* You've knocked down that barrier and are on your way to achieving your goal. But I am not here to lie to you and tell you that everyone can change their life in one simple, swift motion. Admittedly, most of the time it's more difficult than that. Belief systems are like onions, and there are many, many layers to them. Have you ever had a breakthrough that didn't turn out to mean very much in your life? This happens to me all the time. I have a breakthrough, a realization about my behaviors and choices and where they are coming from, and I think, *Whew, I'm so glad I had that breakthrough. I'm not going to have that problem anymore!* And then, soon enough, I'm facing the same problem again.

This happens to all of us. We touch on one of the layers that is causing the belief, but there are deep, deep, hidden layers. Our psyche is so deep that I don't think neuroscience has even scratched the surface of how vast consciousness really is. Some people think that space is the final frontier. I believe it's consciousness. Our consciousness is so vast that we can't necessarily get to the "core belief" every time. And guess what? We don't always have to. Sometimes the best way to get through a barrier belief is to take action anyway.

Let's talk about fear. Fear walks along with our barrier beliefs. I imagine them holding hands, like a soul-crushingly evil couple. Fear gets in the way of *everything*. *Well, I really shouldn't do that because of this or that*, or *I'd love to open my own restaurant, but this, that, and the other are the reasons why it won't work.* You wake up in the middle of the night, or you're taking a shower, and all of a sudden a little idea comes to you. This is a crucial moment. You've just given birth to a new idea. Either you'll take action or you'll talk yourself out of it. And usually you talk yourself out of it, because fear steps in and blocks your path.

This is the most important thing I can tell you: Take action anyway. Even if fear is standing in the way, go ahead. Don't wait. There is a reason you had this thought, this idea. Take action anyway. Stop talking yourself out of it. Just take one little step.

Taking just that one little step in a new direction will open up 10,000 new probabilities for you. Going to that Tony Robbins event certainly opened up 10,000 new probabilities for me. My decision to say to myself that I wanted the next person who called to be happier at the end of the call *absolutely* changed my probabilities in life. Without that choice, my life would be completely different. The truth is that we have no limitations—none—except for the ones that we box ourselves in with. They are all 100 percent self-created.

If you can learn to live 100 percent authentically in choices and behaviors that connect you to the future you want, your life will change so fast you will start using the word *miracle* on a daily basis. Miracles are such easy things to create. You just have to know how to be open to them. And I'm here to help you do that.

CHAPTER 1

CULTIVATING POSITIVE FOCUS

"Whatever we are waiting for—peace of mind, contentment, grace, the inner awareness of Simple Abundance— it will surely come to us, but only when we are ready to receive it with an open and grateful heart."

— SARAH BAN BREATHNACH

In this book you will learn the tools I have gathered through hundreds of hours of therapy, many mistakes, countless pieces of advice, and over 40 years of real-world experience as a business owner, mother of an autistic son, motivational speaker, and constant student of life. This chapter will help you find your focus, identify your gratitude, and unleash your power in order to create the life you have always dreamed of but have never known how to build.

We will start with how my path has unfolded. From the beginning, my life has had its ups and downs, as I'm sure yours has too. But in the interest of focus, I'd like to begin when things were starting to feel good again and the steps I took from that point.

THE EYE OF THE STORM

In the spring of 2007, my future seemed bright, and I couldn't fight the optimism that was seeping into my thoughts. It had been about 10 years since I'd had to bury my first child—my daughter—due to trauma related to her birth. After I recovered from that loss, I married a man who I loved beyond anything I could explain. Together we started our own family, and my business grew alongside our children. It felt, for the first time for as far back as I could remember, like my life was going smoothly.

Our older son, Keagan, had been accepted into a program for gifted and talented students—one that held promise to finally give him the help that I knew he needed. From the time he was very small, he had struggled with communicating verbally, and tantrumed his way through life. Now that he had been admitted to this new school for the fall of 2007, there was hope for a better future—for him and for our family. Keagan was different than other children; he marched to the beat of his own drum, and he was difficult to manage. But he was my son; I loved him, and that was that. By contrast, our younger son, Hayden, was doing very well in school, despite his older brother's behavior issues. By this point my business was well established and growing, and it hummed along like a well-oiled machine.

Apart from testing for admission into the school, the other requirement was that we had to live within the school district. I looked at it as another dream-life manifestation to check off our family's list. With the right planning, we decided, we could upgrade to a newer, more spacious home in a neighborhood within Keagan's new school district. It was my dream house, in every sense of the word, and it matched my dream life that we were slowly but surely creating together.

It was after we had closed on our new dream home that I felt my life shifting. In midspring, my husband transformed before my eyes. The man who had always been a loving, attentive, and generally open-minded man was changing more every day into a nasty, aggressive, and—when he got *really* angry—raging maniac who regularly bullied me into an intimidated, quivering, hysterical mess.

He went from the kind of father who loved hanging out with his kids after work and helping around the house to someone who I couldn't trust. I first knew that there was a problem when he failed to come home one night. This started a spiral of drinking and verbal abuse.

When he was home, he often lost his temper. His rage fests would end with him screaming and yelling, slamming doors, and breaking whatever was within reach. If I called his cell phone when he didn't feel like hearing from me, he would put holes in walls with his bare fists. I loved him and wanted to be a loyal wife, but I felt bullied every single day. There I was, living in my dream house with my two boys and my husband—who I had once adored—all the while living an epic nightmare.

What had gone so terribly wrong?

After a brain scan and psychological visits, my husband was finally diagnosed with bipolar disorder. After a year of treatment, and despite our original commitment of "until death do us part," his bipolar disorder was more than our marriage could survive. It was over.

At the same time as my husband's diagnosis, my older son was also diagnosed with autism and my life felt suffocating and hopeless. On Valentine's Day in 2008, I filed for divorce, and by that August it was final. But it took me another three years to come out on the other side of that war zone in which the boys and I had been living.

Even though I was unsure how to get my life back, I turned myself inside out and examined my belief systems; I asked myself questions about my purpose, about where I was supposed to be, what I should do, and where I should go. I didn't know where any of it would take me, but I'm grateful for it all, because it brought me to today.

CONSCIOUS COMMUNICATIONS

My rock bottom wasn't just a fleeting moment. It was years long. And during those years, I spent some days wondering if my business would collapse, imagining the ways I would end up penniless, disease riddled, and alone. When my mind was idle, I drifted off into dark, unspeakable places and thought about all the other ways my life would end, or worried about how my children would make it without me.

I struggled with identifying and changing my beliefs, but I had a system already tucked into my back pocket. Years before my world began to crumble, I developed a customer-service system called Conscious Communications. It was a simple way for my staff to relate to clients and customers. It was actually so simple that it took the collapse of my life and years of searching for me to see how much power there is in its simplicity.

Through using Conscious Communications, I pulled myself back into the world of the living again. I stopped blaming myself and began choosing to see life through my own personal philosophy. I'd been able to apply this to everyone and everything but myself, but my darkest years became the most fertile soil.

I learned that if you want to change your life—whether big changes or smaller ones—you just have to remember these two things:

1. All it takes to begin (or continue) your journey is a step in the direction of what you want.

2. Every time you make a new choice, you are opening up an infinite number of new opportunities in your life.

During my divorce, I swung between being a functioning catatonic and having a very obvious inner nuclear meltdown. If you'd told me then that total transformation could be simple, and that I could make my life into anything I wanted, I'd have said you were out of your mind.

How could a simple philosophy transform something so complex?

In the healing years that followed the breakdown, I tried everything I could to get well. From traditional talk therapy, Reiki, quantum healing, and shamanic healing to EMDR (eye movement desensitization and reprocessing), Boot Camp for Goddesses®, Tony Robbins, and Joe Dispenza workshops, to retreats in Sedona, at Miraval Resort, and at the Monroe Institute. If it exists, I've probably tried it! Each one had aspects that helped me to heal, and what I learned is that there isn't one magic pill that can do it all. My journey was uphill and steep—like any mountain worth climbing can be—and when I climbed high enough to look at how far I'd come, I was shocked.

I'd been using my own simple principles of taking *one step* in a new direction, every day, to get there; and with each step and choice, I saw life's possibilities opening up before me like never before.

The most surprising thing about changing your world in this way is that the tools to do it are hiding in plain sight, right under your nose, as they say. Once I realized this, it became my new purpose to show others, like you, how to find their inner compass. Each step you take is either getting you closer to or further from your goals or dreams, and with each step comes a whole new set of possible outcomes.

In a graduation speech at the University of the Arts in 2012 (the video of which went viral), English author Neil Gaiman famously inspires graduates to pursue their passions in life in a similar way. Using the metaphor of your goals as mountains, he says, "I knew that as long as I kept walking towards the mountain I would be all right. And when I truly was not sure what to do, I could stop, and think about whether it was taking me towards or away from the mountain." When I watched the YouTube video of this speech, I got chills up and down my whole body because of how aligned it was with my own life philosophy. In it, Gaiman talks about making a personal bucket list of things he wanted to do in his life, and I found myself nodding my head in a powerful agreement. Years before—after my divorce but before I rebounded—I made a list of my biggest desires in life, things that, if they happened, I would attribute to divine magic. It happened that I had eight big desires, so I called the list my Magic 8. In essence, my Magic 8 is a bucket list, but the items are more states of being than milestones, which I also noticed in Gaiman's speech.

The whole speech resonated with me, and I've found alignment with his ideas. Like Gaiman says, the more we pull our focus back onto a path that gets us closer to our personal goals—our mountains—the easier it becomes to live authentically.

We all want to have the ability to change the way we feel, since our feelings determine so much about how we experience our life from day to day. I've found through this work that most people I meet say they just want to be happy. When I learn more about them, though, I hear that they're focused on worry, anger, frustration, or disempowerment, and the list goes on. This creates a superhighway to stress. And their road to joy? It's a bumpy, infrequently traveled dirt road.

I'm going to teach you how to reroute those pathways and to pave that path to joy and happiness so that it, rather than anything else, becomes the default choice. You can prime yourself to feel good. If you already feel good, then you can prime yourself to feel *even better* than you do right now. You do this through exercising that muscle of choice. As with any muscle, you have to make the commitment to strengthen it and keep it active.

I am committed to showing you how to change the way you feel by giving you the tools I've found so far from living through over 40 years on this earth. The countless hours of therapy I've had, the mistakes I've made, the miracles I've witnessed, and the darkest parts of myself all have a purpose now. Even to this day, I'm still healing myself; I'm repairing broken hearts and lines of communication with family and friends, and in some cases, stumbling over something else to work on along the way.

The difference is, now I have a way to live awake and aware, but without the constant suffering. As the Buddha famously said, "Pain is part of life; suffering is optional." Now I truly understand that.

I charted my journey, and from the darkness I traced my way back into a life I could never have imagined possible. And there are still big things that have yet to happen for me. Today I know that they are more than possible; they're *probable*. And I want that same assuredness for you too.

I want to show you that it's possible to make your biggest dreams come true, even if you can't bring yourself to dream anymore. I understand your hesitance.

But I assure you—if I can do it, you can do it too.

UNLEASHING YOUR FOCUS

In 2005 I attended my first Tony Robbins seminar: Unleash the Power Within. I'd learned who Robbins was from a colleague at a Business Networking International meeting, and I felt an enthusiastic curiosity to learn more.

Throughout the event Robbins taught concept after concept that had obvious application to my life—both personal and professional—but two topics in particular stuck with me like glue:

1. Always know your outcome.

2. What you focus on grows.

When I heard Robbins talk about these ideas, it seemed like I'd always known them deep down but hadn't yet defined them. I made the inner connection to these ideas pretty quickly, and I adopted them as though they were mantras.

Always know your outcome.

What you focus on grows.

When you always know your outcome, you are developing the muscle of end-result thinking, which is a mind-set that encourages you to always keep your end-result goals in mind while you're moving throughout life. Strengthening this muscle will, over time, make it easier to identify the *yes* and *no* answers when you're faced with choices, because you'll see what takes you either closer to or further from your desired end result.

When I began noticing how I could apply this concept, I came up with a few practical examples to help illustrate this that I hope you'll find helpful. Before you start something, be it a phone call, a spreadsheet, or homework or an art project with your kids, envision the outcome you desire—without getting caught up in *how* you'll reach that goal. When you envision the end result before you start doing something (or at least near the beginning), your mind works its magic to figure out the best way to get to your intended outcome.

Where you are right now does not matter. The same power that fueled the Wright brothers, Oprah Winfrey, Princess Diana, the young Malala Yousafzai, and even Albert Einstein lies in each and every one of us. This power lies in the thoughts we think each day. According to researcher and best-selling author Joe Dispenza, we think about 60,000 thoughts a day, and 90 to 95 percent of them are the same as yesterday. With this in mind, it stands to reason that the same sequence of thoughts that occurs day in and day out is responsible for the way we regularly think, feel, act, react, speak, and engage with the world—and how we engage with our dreams and goals.

The idea of always knowing your outcome is actually designed to let your brain do what it does best—find solutions to problems. And when we step out of the unconscious, sometimes anxious, worry of *how* we will do something, the brain often comes up with surprising solutions. We must give it the space it needs to sort out the *how*. Most of us set goals for ourselves, such as *lose 20 pounds, become a millionaire, solve department/work problems, start my own business*, or *spend more time with the kids*. Once those goals are set, our programming, which functions like software on a computer, tells us to break the goal down into smaller, actionable steps to help us reach said goal.

What we focus on really does grow. From a perspective that honors the science behind changing our life from the inside out, this means that when you focus on something, your ability to identify and accurately hone in on that very subject becomes sharper. When our brain and environment are in sync, they are *synchronized*. Seeing this connection is called *experiencing*

a synchronicity. Carl Jung originally defined synchronicity as a "meaningful coincidence," and author and philosopher Wayne Dyer said, "Connections and synchronicities are always there—whether we can spot them in the moment or not. This is a Universe where there are no accidents." These synchronicities are controlled by our focus, and the reason what you focus on grows is that the reticular activating system (RAS) in your brain will automatically find matches for your focus—the good or the bad. Our keen sense of identifying what we're focused on over time becomes more heightened. When our focus is in alignment with our outcomes, meaning our thoughts match up with our desires, we become inspired to take new actions, setting in motion thousands of new probabilities.

The reticular activating system is a mechanism in our brain designed to help us find things in our environment that we're focused on. So, for example, if you're trying to get pregnant, all of a sudden you will see babies *everywhere*, and it will seem as though everyone you know is pregnant. Or think about when you buy a new car—you're driving around in your new RAV4, and, *Whoa! There are a lot of RAV4s out on the road today!*

Of course, nothing is new in these situations. Just as many women are pregnant as there were before you became focused on having a baby, and the same number of people own RAV4s as the day before you bought yours. Your RAS is just pointing these things out to you now. The trouble is, it can work against you. If you're focused on something negative, your RAS will take the information that it's given—your focus—and mirror that negativity right back at you, over and over again. When you're having a bad day, a day that starts off poorly and just keeps getting worse—like when you oversleep, and then you're late for work, and then you stub your toe, and then you yell at your kids and pick a fight with your husband—well, you have your RAS to thank for all that.

If you're not sure where your focus is, pay attention to the words that are coming out of your mouth. Following the path of your words will reveal your inner thoughts, which are a reflection of your focus. What are the things you repetitively and unconsciously say? If you hear yourself say, *I'm a mess*, or *I'm so stressed out*, this outer dialogue is probably a reflection of your inner feelings. Think about phrases like *Oh, this always happens to me!* or *I am a horrible test taker*, or *I'll be single forever!* or *I can't lose weight; I've tried everything!* All these statements reflect a focus and its matching thought pattern. For example, *I am a horrible test taker* is a reflection of low confidence or not believing in yourself—it really doesn't have anything to do with whether you've done poorly on tests in the past or not. Cognitive bias studies even show that test results are better for people who are told they will do better. Believing that they will do better means that they actually get better scores.

YOUR FOCUS DETERMINES YOUR DRIVE

So how do you get that reticular activating system working *for* you instead of against you? Remember that you are the boss of your own RAS—you just have to tell it what to do. And you do that by consciously choosing what to focus on. Your RAS basically functions like a bouncer at the door to your mind. If you deliberately choose your focus (that is, determine who is on the guest list), your RAS will let in only who you say can get in.

Of course it can be hard to ensure that you're always focusing only on the positive. We all slide into negative thinking sometimes. The best way to pull yourself out of that hole is to concentrate on the end result. Using end-result thinking as your guidepost pointing toward where you want to go creates opportunities that will surprise you, since it engages the creative centers of the brain and encourages them to navigate those unknown waters for you in masterful ways. I use *end result* interchangeably with *dream* and *goal*, because the way I see it, they're all referring to the hope you're reaching for. And this is what cultivating positive focus is all about.

Whether your dream is to be a multimillionaire or your greatest joy is being a full-time mom, *dream* works for you as whatever you want it to be. Sometimes your dreams include awards, prestige, and achievement; and other times it's the opposite. Whether it's to be President, to run a marathon, or to have a pleasant experience while caring for your aging parents, *or just to be happy,* when you are focused on the end result, you will be more likely to get your life in alignment with it.

Inside the brain, your focus encourages certain synapses to fire, producing a clear picture of what you want your end result to be, and allowing the brain to produce actionable steps that feel like intuitive guidance. Your approach to finding clarity should be simple, because once you inch toward complexity, your mind is moving toward chaos. When it comes to your big-picture goals for your life, know this: clarity is simple; complexity is chaos.

The more complex you make something, the more impossible it will seem, as it breeds a feeling of impossibility. On the other hand, clarity breeds a feeling of infinite probabilities. Can you imagine what it will feel like to know how many things are possible for you, instead of focusing on what you think is *im*possible?

I'd like to pause here for some reflection and have you ask yourself the following questions. Your answers to these are indicators for the tone of how you react to other scenarios with which you are faced.

1. *During times of crisis, am I focused on the problem or the solution?*

2. *Do I imagine worst possible outcomes? Do I ever ask myself, what is the worst thing that could happen?* (Hint: when you ask and answer this question realistically, it will usually defuse the anxiety to a more reasonable and appropriate level for the situation at hand.)

3. *What is my possible solution? How can I focus on that instead of the problem?*

4. *What can I do about this?* (Instead of thinking of all the things you *can't* do.)

How did your answers sound? While it's not black and white (and rarely is anything *ever* that), reflecting on our behavior and reactions around crises often tells us more about where we're unconsciously putting our focus even when things are not in a state of alarm.

As Eric Barker of *Time* magazine put it, "You create your world with what you pay attention to." Regardless of whether your focus is negative or positive, whatever you regularly turn your attention and focus toward will cause your brain's RAS to search for and seek out matching material. So if you go to a cocktail party that you didn't really want to go to and you have a terrible experience, it might be because your brain has been given the memo to look for evidence to support the fact that you will not have a good time: the food is too cold, the music is too loud, and there is no one interesting to talk to. Complaints like these will reinforce your belief that you're going to have a terrible time at the next party too.

The same kind of cause and effect happens if you're speaking about positive things or being grateful for the good in your life. If these things already exist in your world, your awareness will be heightened so you'll notice more and more of those good things . . . and if there's an absence of the good you speak of, your subconscious will create the circumstances for you so that it will be able to notice more of those good things, thereby satisfying the work order you put in place with your words. Cool, right?

What we talk about is what we are thinking about. What we are thinking about is what we are focused on, and what we are focused on becomes the story we tell—which is a feedback loop. We'll talk more about feedback loops in later chapters, but my mission is to help you see how your focus determines so much of your life experience.

This is the seed of truth that declares the most thrilling fact known to humankind: you can change your reality with just your words.

PUTTING THE LESSONS INTO ACTION

Once I understood these concepts, I decided I was going to put them into action at the office. I was so inspired to believe something different was possible that I made a list of my personal and professional intentions for focus, as well as my goals, so that I could teach what I'd learned to my staff . . . and I was eager to get it going.

I found myself regurgitating many of the things that Robbins had taught at his seminar. I impressed even myself with how inspirational I sounded when talking to my staff. Still, though, I stuttered on phone calls. I wanted them to go differently, to *feel* different . . . but I didn't know how to make that happen. I noticed how heated I became in the face of conflict or how I triggered conversations with customers and I didn't like it. So, to address this, I called a meeting to recalibrate with my staff.

I'd been preaching the importance of end-result thinking for the last several weeks, and I still sensed something missing from my leadership and execution of this idea. Hence my struggle to make it through conversations with customers without feeling a competition between my internal drive to win and my desire for everyone to feel calm and satisfied.

I picked up a dry-erase marker and began to speak. "Okay, team. Let's pick an outcome for today's training."

By that statement alone, it was obvious I was flying by the seat of my pants, but they trusted me. I drew in a breath and then it happened . . . because I had intended to find the missing piece (my end result), the more abstract creativity centers in my brain kicked into gear, and before I knew it, I blurted out a statement that I'd have never approved my conscious mind to say, which was: "I want the next person who calls to be happier by the end of the call than they were when they called in. I don't want to worry about whether or not they paid the bill . . . I only want to make them less frustrated and more happy." I paused. "How does that sound?"

I heard my own voice. *How did that sound?* It sounded crazy! This was a collection agency, not a spa! And yet . . . it was right. I'd never thought of it before that moment, but suddenly I wanted to experiment to see if we could make it work. Plus, I wondered if achieving that goal more regularly would increase my staff's success rates, considering that happy people were always more inclined to cooperate.

We sat in silence for only another moment or so before the phone rang. A nervous smile spread across my face. Just like you'd imagine it in a movie, my staff huddled around the conference table in the small conference room, leaning in as I put the call on speakerphone and answered it. "Thank you for calling Midstate Collection Solutions. This is Mary; how can I help you?"

I had always associated myself with Julia Sugarbaker's alter ego, the Terminator, from *Designing Women,* and I was often proud of how powerful that role made me feel. But once my conscious mind caught up to the bright idea of making the customer happier, my subconscious set in motion the transition from the domineering Terminator to the sweet Julia Sugarbaker.

I sailed through that call, faking the enthusiasm of a cheerleader, my staff listening intently as I tried to make that customer happy.

"I'm happy to get that information for you!" I enthusiastically responded when the customer requested more information on her account about halfway through the call. There was a familiar sensation coursing through my body—the rush of adrenaline I got whenever I faced a challenge. Did that customer have a life-changing phone call? Probably not. But I did.

So with "customer happiness" as my new North Star, we carried on, and it wasn't long before we evolved our employee training manual and created the Do Not Say list. Because I learned how to use Conscious Communications to help alleviate the burden of debt, our company grew 33 percent that year. Intentional focus and end-result thinking began to leave powerful marks not only on my staff's professional performance and personal lives, but on nearly every aspect of my life too.

DEVELOPING THE ATTITUDE OF GRATITUDE

I can probably guess what you are thinking. You're thinking that all this sounds great, but changing your brain or creating new neural pathways has to be difficult. The great news is that it's much easier than you think. Believe me, I didn't always know how easy it truly was. This may surprise you, but since the dawn of consciousness, ancient sages, monks, priests, and contemporary teachers, guides, scientists, and leaders all say the same thing: Developing an active, daily gratitude practice changes brain chemistry. It changes the ways our genes express themselves in our body, and it fundamentally rewrites old scripts in our brain that we are ready to be done with.

Being grateful is a state of mind. And this mind-set only regularly exists when you make a habit of noticing the good things in your life. By identifying what you're grateful for, you're training your RAS to look for things in your world to support that state of mind. In 2003 American researchers Robert Emmons and Michael McCullough tested this theory by instructing one group of participants to write in a gratitude journal for 10 weeks, while other groups wrote about their annoyances or about neutral life events. They found that the participants who expressed their gratitude daily showed increases in overall well-being compared to the other groups. In my experience finding little things to be grateful for is a quick way to feel better. And when you feel better, you can choose even better or bigger things to be grateful for— including things that haven't happened yet.

Affirmations are nearly identical in function to gratitude. But when you're feeling low or when you can't see past a difficult or traumatic event, it feels like a lie to stare at yourself in the mirror and affirm something like *I love being a multimillionaire!* or *My body is strong and healthy!* or *Every day, in every way, I'm getting happier, healthier, and wiser!* Being grateful for what *is* true, on the other hand, pulls you more quickly out of the muck. It lets you notice the joy of your soft pillow, the sound of birds chirping in the morning, a baby giggling at the park during your lunch break, or a relaxing night in with your favorite movie and a glass of wine.

For a moment I'd like you to imagine what it might look like inside your brain when you practice being grateful for something small instead of slipping into complaining about something that might be equally small in importance. Consider the difference between *I am so grateful I have a roommate who helps pay the bills* and *It's so annoying when my roommate leaves the television on all day*. Neither thought will immediately make or break your physical reality, but wherever you put your attention—on the negative thought or the grateful one—will literally change your brain to strengthen the connection to one state of mind or the other.

Habits don't form overnight. In fact, health psychology researcher Phillippa Lally found that establishing a new habit can take anywhere from 18 to 254 days, but generally takes 66 days to fully form and become truly habitual. Replacing your negative thoughts with positive ones may take time, but the practice of gratitude can act like Scrubbing Bubbles for the negativity in your brain. They work hard so you don't have to.

From here on out in this book, I'm asking you to trust me. Trust that each of these exercises is intended to guide you toward repatterning and reprogramming your brain so that you can achieve more of what you want in life and less of what you don't. If you can honor this agreement while working your way through the book, and as you complete the small, actionable, and achievable tasks that I give you—even if you are skeptical—I promise you'll start changing your life. And it'll more than likely be an even better change than you might have hoped for.

Do we have a deal?

CULTIVATING GRATITUDE

Around the time best-selling author Pam Grout was launching her book *E Squared*, I found myself in a scary emotional place after the end of a romantic relationship. The pain felt as real as an open wound, and my despair around how the relationship had ended was as big as the sadness. I knew I needed to do something—*anything*—to change my focus, but I was so low that I couldn't see how it was even possible.

When I watched an interview with Grout, I heard only what I needed to hear in that moment, and that was about her dedication to practicing gratitude every single day.

That triggered a suppressed truth in me, and I remembered that the foundation of all the things I'd learned over the years is gratitude. Gratitude wasn't something that initially came easily or naturally to me, but Grout's dedication to her gratitude practice inspired me to create my own.

I formed a Facebook gratitude group with friends and strangers, and to this day the first three women who responded to my request are still in my gratitude group, which is now called Declaring Gratitude. Every day we text each other three specific things we are grateful for. Not only has it changed my life, but it has changed the lives of the others in my group too. It's the one daily practice that we never let slip. One friend in particular, Victoria, was a corporate attorney for Yahoo. Her life was "successful" in just about every way that most people define success—but Victoria came to realize that *she* didn't define success that way. All she wanted was to live a life surrounded by love and grace. She took a huge leap and moved to Australia to explore life in a commune. The gratitude group wasn't the only thing that held her true to her decision, but it helped! And more than that, our focus on gratitude created a shift for each of us, as we all took huge leaps forward in our lives. As Victoria says, that's no coincidence. We've continued to send one another our gratitude lists every day since January 2015, and this one addition to my life has become the very framework for how I can maintain my focus and always know (and focus on) my desired outcomes.

From everything I've gone through, learned, witnessed, and been part of over the years, I can say with confidence that the starting place for changing your life is gratitude. Even Harvard Medical School has published studies on gratitude, and in 2011 reported that "gratitude is strongly and consistently associated with greater happiness." And as researchers Emmons and McCullough found, simple expressions of it can bring about greater overall life satisfaction. Gratitude is the foundation of personal development, as it is the daily activity behind precisely how you are rewiring your brain's pathways and programming. In fact, the fastest way to influence your creative imagination is with gratitude. All the great thinkers, teachers, leaders, business-people, and visionaries throughout history have insisted as much.

Imagine one morning when you wake up in a bad mood, yet because of your committed gratitude practice, you have to find something to be grateful for. I imagine you'd find your point of gratitude, whether you liked it or not, and you would go about starting your day. If you stubbed your toe one morning, what if instead of cursing you said how grateful you were that your toe wasn't broken? Well, doing so would pivot your attitude away from your bad mood and toward gratefulness. It would change your focus, output, and outlook for the entire day. Imagine the benefits of sending positive ripple effects out from where you are that will move you closer to where you want to be. This simple practice could change the way you live, helping you find more meaning, happiness, and joy in the everyday. Who wouldn't want to welcome this type of change into their lives? I know I would.

Science confirms that gratitude changes the foundation of our attitude, shifting us more toward optimism than pessimism, which then translates into a greater ability to both dream and *act* on our dreams.

Since this is so, doesn't it seem like some gratitude is in order?

EXERCISE: YOUR GRATITUDE GROUP

Find at least two friends with whom you can digitally communicate your gratitude list *every day*. Aim to share at least three things you are grateful for with each other daily, and send those gratitudes to your partners through either e-mail or text. Based on trial and error, I recommend that you try to send your gratitudes to each other early in the day, as setting your intentions for your day with a practice of gratitude will lead to feeling better throughout your day. But there's no *wrong* way to be grateful! Even if you forget to send your list early in the day, just try to remember that gratitude can reset the mind at *any time of day*. Don't stop yourself from the benefits of expressing gratitude just because it didn't turn out in the way you hoped it would when you rolled out of bed that morning.

Once you've established your gratitude group, set your intention to utilize this gratitude practice to activate small pivots toward more happiness in your morning and throughout your day. You'll be surprised: when you know that what you focus on grows, and you redirect your focus to three new things you're grateful for each day—and you share them with at least two other people to keep yourself accountable to the practice— good things will come to pass for you.

When you have even the littlest bit of evidence for how gratitude is making your days feel better, please hop on over to the Facebook group (www.facebook.com/groups/ gratitudegirlsgroup) and let me know how your gratitude is affecting your life. I'd love to hear from you!

Now that you've established what you are grateful for, we can dig into what you want to change in your life. In the next chapter, you will learn how to heal your wounds by rewriting your story. You will also learn what your barrier beliefs are and how to eliminate them. Chapter 2 will help you understand why your brain is the way it is, while teaching you how to change your neural pathways to create the version of yourself that you have always wanted to be.

TAKE YOUR BRAIN TO LUNCH: HOW TO REWRITE YOUR BELIEFS AND SKYROCKET YOUR VALUE

"Progress is impossible without change, and those who cannot change their minds cannot change anything."

— GEORGE BERNARD SHAW

Now that you know a bit about me and a bit more about yourself, your desires, and how to develop an attitude of gratitude, we will focus on identifying the beliefs that may be limiting you. In this chapter you will learn how to clean your "lenses of perception" and build a new mind-set.

HEALING MY LIFE

After the dust settled from my divorce, I reached a point where the story I was telling had become so familiar that I didn't see how painful or destructive it was. That pattern had become my new normal. I grew my business with unparalleled success, and we expanded in rapid ways, but I was numb on the inside. Without realizing it I'd come to believe that my signature system only worked on other people.

One evening in 2012, I drew a hot bath for myself, carefully climbed in, and opened YouTube. One of my favorite things to do is soak in a hot bath and learn about things I'm fascinated by on YouTube. Because that platform is "smart," learning your preferences and suggesting videos based on past videos you've liked, I got it to the point where I would watch whatever video it suggested next. It always inspired me.

Louise Hay's film *You Can Heal Your Life* came up as a suggested video, and I clicked PLAY. I had never heard of Louise Hay, Hay House, or the film before, but by the end of the opening scene, I had dissolved into a rainforest of tears.

In the first scene, a woman in the car berates and bullies herself in unspoken but pervasively critical ways. She says things like:

- *I'm so stupid.*
- *I hate this.*
- *I'm such an idiot.*
- *I always do this.*
- *Why did I take the 580? I'm going to be late.*
- *I look like the walking dead . . .*
- *Why am I always acquiescing to everyone?*

My heart swelled with such grief; I felt like I *was* that woman! The film touched parts of myself I'd hidden even *from* myself. I couldn't explain how I'd avoided seeing how wounded I was, but how could I deny what had hit my heart so directly? I cried for the whole 90-minute film, sobbing into the truths it exposed. I'd been found out—those feelings of shame and guilt around my daughter's death, the humiliation and feelings of being shattered by my divorce, and my overall general sense of unworthiness around love, family, and connection.

The bathwater had gone cold and my fingertips were like withered raisins as I wiped my cheeks at the end of the movie.

Then I got out of the tub like a lightning bolt. I was ready, in that moment, to reclaim my life, and I instantly decided I was going to write a book. A kind of excitement pulsed through my body as I dried off, announcing to my empty bathroom: "Louise Hay is going to publish my book someday." As if my body had been jolted forward with electricity, I called a friend to talk to her about my book idea, and I confidently told her Louise Hay was going to publish it. There weren't any doubts in my mind at all. I found that pulse of possibility in my own life again.

I danced around my bathroom, and reveled in the hope that everything was going to be okay. I even got a glimpse of where I am today. It was at that moment that I knew something magical was possible, because I related to the woman's journey in the movie. I felt like I had just opened the door to the possibility of change. I instantly realized that I had already done all this work; I just needed to get back to it.

Within a few days of my watching that film, everyone around me knew who Louise Hay was. I bought every copy of the film on Amazon and eBay, and everyone—from friends to fitness instructors to strangers—got a copy of *You Can Heal Your Life*. I passed the DVDs out like candy on Halloween.

Looking back, I realize why the film had such a profound impact on me. To survive traumas in life is one thing; I had that skill down. But to actually rebound, recover, and *thrive* after trauma is another thing altogether. I was a survivor, but I wasn't thriving. And I definitely hadn't recovered. While the devastation and betrayal that went along with my divorce felt like a huge inciting event, the truth that my limiting beliefs went much deeper than that recent series of events stared me right in the face.

It was no wonder the movie brought me to a place where I sobbed uncontrollably.

The movie also helped me uncover a massive list of limiting beliefs I needed to work through, which I might not have ever learned about had I not watched it. In fact, I would go as far as to say that my limiting beliefs weren't just limiting me; they were like a brick wall, making me barricade everything deep, meaningful, or interesting in life, and I hadn't even been aware of their existence merely hours before seeing the film. This realization made me aware that the work I'd been doing at the office—the creation, training, and use of Conscious Communications—actually did apply to my personal life. In short, it gave me that thread of hope that I *could* get back to who I knew I was deep down at the core of myself. Before I'd gotten pummeled by life, I always spoke proudly of my dreams, aspirations, and life's purpose, but I'd lost touch with that woman.

There was a time in my life when I had boldly framed and shared my ambitions with anyone who would listen, but after each obstacle, after the weights piled higher onto me, I adapted to the hand I was dealt—though it wasn't pretty. I became a master at surviving within a whole spectrum of chaotic circumstances, but instead of feeling strong or resilient, I found myself totally devoid of self-worth. Everything I did in my personal life seemed to reinforce the limiting belief that I wasn't worthy.

I began identifying the stories that kept me swirling in that limiting belief of worthlessness.

The obstacles that were holding me back were true obstacles only because I *believed* them to be true. My beliefs about and interpretation of myself were what determined how I felt about myself, and only I could change that. I knew I had work to do to truly recover and thrive.

This was a challenge in the best way possible; it was time I learned how to love myself again, and I was ready to get started.

RE-CREATING YOUR STORY

As you've likely experienced in your own life, when we get together with other people, the most effective way we connect and relate to one another is through sharing stories. These stories, and the words that fill in their details, are incredibly powerful. Over time our stories become our identities. Stories are powerful! Any story we tell can either make us feel great or make us feel awful, even if the story is about someone else. When it comes to our own life, we have the choice: Our stories can make us feel powerful or powerless. We get to decide the stories we tell and how we tell them.

The idea is not to repress or ignore anything that's happened to you if it makes you feel bad, and I'm not here to encourage you to pretend to be someone you're not. But you *do* have options for how you want to perceive your life and your story. Why not try telling a story from your life that makes you feel good instead of one that makes you feel sick to your stomach?

In my own life, I have learned to choose to celebrate the good that has happened, but that doesn't mean I've had a particularly charmed life. In fact, it was quite the opposite. It's taken a great deal of serious work for me to view what's happened to me in ways that acknowledge my personal motion forward, rather than feeling stuck in my own victimhood. This internal pivot isn't an easy thing for people to see from the outside, but I bring it up because no one among us can skate through life without loss, grief, disappointment, anger, despair, and the list goes on. Just like the saying goes: it's not what happens to you that matters, it's *how you see what happens to you* that matters. This is a universal truth, through and through.

While I'll never be able to unexperience a challenge, there are traumatic memories that are so difficult to recall that remembering them is like watching a somewhat familiar movie on a screen made of burlap. As is true for most of us, my early years weren't easy—but giving attention and focus to the memories of instability and darkness during those times won't do me any good today.

I didn't come to this awareness through osmosis or because I'm so full of virtue that it just dawned on me out of the blue. I got here because, when I was going through my divorce—which was as painful and drawn out as I could have imagined in my wildest nightmare—I finally hit the bottom of what I thought was a bottomless pit. It was a dark and emotionally destructive place, and I wanted out of that pit. That was it. I was sick and tired of feeling sick and tired, and I wanted to feel better. I wanted to get relief from the grief and inner struggle I felt, so I finally reached out for help.

That help took shape as I landed in the office of a therapist who used EMDR as his primary tool to help patients speed up their healing process. It was in that therapy that I was first able to interrupt the pattern of feeling victimized—or rather, it was when the pattern was interrupted *for* me. Literally every time I started to tell (or retell) my therapist one of my victim stories, he gently cut me off. In truth, I was relieved; the last thing I wanted was to waste time and money repeating the same stories, week after week—despite the habit I'd made of swirling around that pain.

Within that first session, my therapist redirected me more times than I could count. After the first handful of times, I saw what was happening: in those moments, he was preventing me from identifying with a story that disempowered me, cutting off a pathway in my brain that only contributed to more heartache. Witnessing this happen to me, and watching my therapist use this tool on me, was profoundly impactful. Eventually that process helped me see that everything I needed to heal myself was actually within me already, and it had been the whole time.

Through witnessing my own negative pattern interruptions in the moment and observing what they did within my body, mind, and interactions with other people, I also found out that I was (and still am) the only one with the power to pull myself out of that pit. From being abandoned as a child to losing a child of my own when I was 20 years old, up through a humiliating and reality-altering divorce, I had a lot to recover from. It was not an easy process, and the more I committed to healing, the more I realized that I was—and still am—on a *journey* of healing. There is no official destination to reach on this healing journey, just a path toward mindfulness and living in the present.

As I've moved forward and re-created my story, I've paid attention to what worked and what didn't, and to other tools that worked for others but not myself. I'm beside myself with gratitude that through what I've experienced I have been able to gather up those tools and bits of wisdom, if for no other reason than that I can relay them to you, as you too learn to heal.

Being in that therapeutic environment was an important starting point for me. Before that experience I had been stuck in a disempowering story that I hadn't even realized had a hold on me. I feel it's important to restate that there is no such thing as a "right" or "only" starting point on your journey to healing. When you can identify a limiting belief that you're no longer willing to co-sign, *how* you let it go doesn't matter as much as *that* you let it go.

What I did—and continue to do and teach others to do—was to find a pathway *around* the old pattern or belief, rather than tracking back through the old wounds each time and letting my boots get caked with the mud of a story that doesn't serve me anymore.

The story of my childhood was one I found myself telling often. By the time I was six, I'd been shuffled around between family members more times than I can count. My parents broke up before I learned to talk, and I didn't have a relationship with my biological father. In fact, I knew only that his job title was "nuclear engineer," which sounded important. After my parents' divorce, my mother became unstable to the point that my sister and I were temporarily moved to a relative's house.

Eventually my mother found the strength within to return to the role in which I knew her: mom. But she came with the addition of my new stepfather, Alex, a man I had never met before.

Then came the hardest news: I was moving back in with my mother, but my sister would stay with our relatives. I was devastated. Even at six years old, I wondered with all my heart whether I'd ever be able to trust anything or anyone again. There was an obvious feeling of abandonment at a very early age, but it was a displaced feeling that I always traced back to missing my best friend—my little sister—even after Alex and my mother had a son.

My childhood was filled with ups and downs due to my mother's bipolar disorder (only later diagnosed), her remarriage, my heartbreaking separation from my sister at a young age, and eventually the introduction of a new bundle of joy, my baby brother.

I tell you this to illustrate the paradox of my story—and every human's story too. Our stories are important, and yet they're not important in the way we think they are. On the one hand, we understand who we are through stories. We tell each other stories at get-togethers with loved ones, in front of acquaintances or co-workers at parties or networking events, and we find meaning by connecting with each other through our shared stories. On the other hand, while this makes us feel better temporarily, that feeling fades when we realize that now the other person sees us through the lens of that story we just told them. We like feeling connected—but this isn't the enriching kind of connection. These kinds of exchanges actually *dis*connect us from the life of our dreams by pulling us back into the past.

When we relive our stories again and again, it keeps us swirling in those stories—in the past. If we swirl inside the painful stories of our past, what we're doing in the present is creating more stories that disconnect us from our desired futures. What if instead we dwelled in the story that makes us feel good, that inspires us, and that connects us to the magic in life?

In the book *Wild*, best-selling author Cheryl Strayed calls her backpack "Monster"—a fitting name for the baggage she carries with her on her months-long hike up the Pacific Crest Trail. What we repeatedly tell ourselves becomes our beliefs and subconscious programming . . . these are often the monsters that slow us down, much like Strayed's physical backpack named Monster, weighing heavily on our physical, emotional, and mental energies. Our conscious and subconscious programming is with us in every moment of every day; any glitches in our programming—any monsters we don't keep in line—will effectively disconnect us from our desired outcomes in life.

You know that story you've believed that your parents loved your sibling more than you? Or the one where your first husband cheated and was a controlling jerk? Or perhaps your story is worse, and involves years of childhood trauma and abuse. No matter what the painful narrative is, that story becomes the monster that you carry around on your back, the glitch in your brain's software that prevents you from being your most alive self.

The problem of being so identified with our stories is that the more we tell a particular story of abandonment, abuse, neglect, or trauma, the heavier our monster-backpack becomes—and the more disconnected we become from our dreams.

I know how hard it is to find a new way to frame the truth of our tragedies; I've had to work at it myself, and I continue to do so. It helps to practice with smaller stories of woe or even complaints. These can act like a traffic jam and are worth reframing simply because of the way those stories impact how we feel from moment to moment, which in turn impacts how we view our life.

At any point in the narrative of your life, you can find another entrance to your story. In any moment, you can start to reprogram your belief systems, loosen your grip on the past, and cast your conscious focus toward your desires . . . and you can do it by starting with just a few words.

CLEANING YOUR GLASSES

About a year ago in my yoga practice, I learned about the concept of *avidya*, which is a Vedic Sanskrit word meaning "to be ignorant" or "to see something through a lens of misperception." When we misperceive our realities—whether we're putting on our rose-colored glasses or our smudged glasses—we don't see ourselves or the world as they really are.

Women especially are regularly encouraged to *chin up, stop complaining, put our big girl pants on,* or *settle* for what we know deep down isn't right. Through this settling we dim our light and accumulate more smudges and smears on the lens of how we see ourselves and our life. The lens of misperception, avidya, keeps us buried beneath layers of untruths, away from seeing things as they really are, and as they could be.

When I teach workshops about personal empowerment, I regularly reference the idea of cleaning the smudged lens of our perception. We need to become aware of our avidya and clean off that lens of our ingrained beliefs. Doing so is freeing, but first we've got to be willing to acknowledge that the smudge on our lens exists.

Life can be much easier when we learn to see things as they really are. While it's important to be open to possibilities and to speak positive things about ourselves, it is also important to be honest. When we see things as better than they are, it only gives us temporary relief from discomfort, and we may end up ignoring our problems without finding solutions. When we see things as worse than they are, we exaggerate our pain, which keeps us swirling at the bottom of that pit.

Do you want to make better decisions and take massive action in the direction of your dreams? Then choose to see things as they really are. It is *this* that allows for the supercharged clarity you'll need to make things happen.

How you choose to look back on your past (your lens of perception) will either connect or disconnect you from the future of your dreams. But our lenses are so familiar that even if we're in pain, there's resistance to letting go of the misperception that is causing the pain. When we lessen our emotional attachment to unpleasant or painful memories—and maybe even inch toward forgiveness little by little—we can burn off the misperceptions, create new neural pathways and beliefs, and make way for bigger and better things, like more loving connections, more success, and more vitality.

How do you do this?

Create a new story. Or, rather, start by changing the way you *tell* your story.

YOUR MANIPULATED MEMORY

While there may be times that we feel victimized when we recall a traumatic memory, having that memory in and of itself is a primal instinct to help us avoid walking into danger twice. Just imagine if we never remembered that a hot stove could burn us. Our memories are key for survival, but when it comes to reliving painful memories, our brain can supercharge the emotional attachment to a memory in such a way that even having that memory feels more like a liability than an asset.

It's important to mention here that memory is subjective, and that two people can see the same event from the same vantage point and recall it very differently. We can all remember at least one family function where relatives told contradicting versions of the same story, can't we? This just confirms what science substantiates time and again: many of the memories we recall are not accurate.

There's a reason for this: inside each memory is an associated emotion, which is unique to every person. Neuroscientist Paul King found that: "Memories are stored as microscopic chemical changes at the connection points between neurons in the brain." When you recall a memory, your brain is programmed to release a specific set of chemicals into your nervous system to either cheer you up or send you into a spiral of discomfort or unhappiness, depending on that emotion's associated intensity. If you change the feelings associated with the memory, you change the chemistry, and by default, you change your life. Being able to enact this type of change is groundbreaking and simple, and I'm going to show you how to do it.

In order to create a new belief, we must be willing to reframe our attachments to memories. This means making a change in the emotional association we have with a memory. Let's move in the direction of creating a new life by changing our thoughts, beliefs, and actions—things we can do *today*.

TOOLS FOR REFRAMING

Step 1. Stop hitting the PLAY button on your repetitive, tragic stories. They disconnect you from your dreams, and retelling a story only strengthens its neural pathways, which strengthens the emotional attachment to the memory, and re-creates the chemical recipe in your body to match the original emotions of the trauma. This can actually cause you to become addicted to your stories—especially if they get you sympathy or attention. Both of these results give you more fuel to relive the emotions of a story, which tells your brain to put out more matching chemicals. Telling an emotional story may make you feel connected to whoever you're venting to, but it's not a healthy connection. Some venting is fine—get whatever it is off your chest, a few times if you need to—but then make your pivot.

Step 2. Loosen your grip on the traumatic emotional injuries of your past. When you stop repeating a story over and over, it will help you loosen your grip. Another way to loosen your grip is to make a list of how the painful experience or trauma strengthened you. Remember that *what you focus on grows*, so by lessening your attachment to the trauma and focusing on how you're stronger now, you can begin to focus on something else, like your dreams and desires.

Step 3. Tell a new story. I'm not suggesting you lie, but instead of telling the story of trauma, consciously choose to tell your triumph stories more than your traumas. Use *words that work* to create a new chapter in your life. Talk about your highest desires and what you can do to get there. Again, *what you focus on grows,* so telling the stories of what you want to come to pass will point your focus toward a brand-new destination.

The process outlined above is designed to help you shed the disempowering negative emotions associated with your memories, for no other reason than to set you free. It was when I started loosening my grip on the emotions I attached to certain memories that I learned it was the *intensity* of the emotional response to each memory that determined how much pain I'd feel or how strong the associated belief would be.

MY OWN TRAGEDY (AND HOW I REFRAMED IT)

Choosing to not dwell on past traumas doesn't mean never talking about them again. When I got pregnant with my first child, I was terrified. At 19 years old, I went to college part time and worked part time, but my boyfriend and I were textbook poor, living paycheck to paycheck in a 10-foot by 50-foot trailer and barely making it. Times were as tough as I thought they would ever be, and getting pregnant compounded our fears about how we would ever be able to support a child when we could barely support ourselves. My optimism kept me clinging to hope, but I had to acknowledge that optimism itself wasn't enough to put food on the table.

When I went into labor, something went very wrong. My baby underwent such trauma during labor that she had to be resuscitated at birth. The doctors described it as the equivalent of her having spent five minutes at the bottom of a pool—essentially asphyxiating—and then being brought back to life. They warned us she may have brain damage. But in that moment, we couldn't do anything but rejoice; we were so relieved our child lived. We named her Haley.

Once Haley was stable, the doctors discovered that because she'd been without oxygen for so long, she had indeed suffered severe brain damage. They told us that she would never recover from her vegetative state. I look at pictures of myself during that time, and it seemed like I too was a vegetable. I was listless, I hardly smiled, and it felt like I had lost access to whatever personal momentum I had before the trauma of Haley's birth. She looked so much like every other typically developed baby that I had ever seen that I couldn't help but be in denial. How could it be true that she would never rebound? I believed that my love would heal my daughter, if nothing else would.

It turned out that it didn't matter how much love I gave or how much hope I had that she would come out of it one day. Caring for an incapacitated infant whose brain would not develop was a never-ending nightmare. And as the relationship with my boyfriend disintegrated, it became a nightmare that I suddenly found myself facing alone. I watched her scream and suffer as I suctioned her lungs to remove pooling fluid multiple times a day. I fed her through a surgically implanted permanent gastronomy tube in her belly, and I administered countless doses of seriously scary medications, like phenobarbital and valium, to prevent seizures and lessen her pain. As much as I tried, there was nothing I could do to completely erase her pain. Eighteen months after she was born, Haley died from complications of the myriad health issues she fought. I was distraught, confused, and hopeless at losing her, while simultaneously feeling relief for the end of her suffering, and mine. It was the perfect situation for me to unknowingly cultivate a powerful story of guilt and shame.

But instead, through this experience, I realized just how much I was capable of. While Haley was alive, I had become obsessed with learning about the brain. I threw myself back into school full time, I worked part time at the school library through a work-study program, I found a special needs day care for while I was in school or at work, and I was able to take Haley back and forth from the hospital every month—which was a two-hour drive each way. In all this I saw just how much perseverance, strength, and tenacity I had. While the experience taxed me more than I could acknowledge at the time, it also set into motion my desire to learn about the brain. In many ways my desire to understand and help my daughter heal offset my focus from swirling in the trauma, and instead I focused on searching for a solution.

In my research I learned about some incredible scientific developments within the realm of stem cell research. At the time it was more theoretical than practical—and we were still decades away from using stem cell treatments on patients. Even though we couldn't heal Haley's brain, through this period I unknowingly began to heal my own traumas. I began realizing how strong I am and discovering that my interests were in learning about the brain. And in time I would come to see how my choice to focus on finding a solution instead of dwelling on the problem may have been a key ingredient for why, when Haley did die, I didn't die with her. Instead, I carried on.

Dropping out of college after Haley died, I found a job at a bank. But it turned out that, while I loved working at the bank, I was a much better boss than employee—and the boss's job wasn't exactly up for grabs.

Although now I see it as the best thing that ever happened to me, at the time getting fired from a dream job on the heels of rebounding from the loss of my daughter sent me lower than I thought possible. After that I took the first job I was offered, and that was to work as a telemarketer. I didn't have time to rationalize or think my way out of it. I needed to feed, clothe, and shelter myself.

During this time I struggled to recover my self-image, since I didn't have a family, a college degree, or much direction. On a personal level, I felt like a loser, but despite my ongoing internal existential identity crisis, I excelled at work.

Because of the small positive improvement in my days based on my job performance, it didn't take long before the fog lifted a little here and a little there, helping me see more clearly each day. I worked at the telemarketing job for three years, and it had an enormous impact on me. In fact, that experience is what taught me that sometimes we unknowingly get put into situations that become fundamentally important to us later in life.

THE SCIENCE BEHIND OUR BELIEF SYSTEMS

Our emotional connection to people, circumstances, and events affects what we believe. Through my research I have found that, unlike other animals, humans develop their belief systems in three often interchangeable but distinct ways:

1. By learning from and observing our families

2. By learning through our early childhood experiences

3. By participating in our culture and community

This is how our total environment makes up our belief systems. Seeing how broad this is, let's look at how neural pathways are created and how belief systems are born.

If you can, picture an image of a brain whose neural networks are lit up, with blue impulses moving swiftly through its circuitry. In that brain there are hundreds of billions of neurons, and in between each neuron is a gap, which is called a synapse. When the brain has a thought, an electrical impulse moves from one neuron to the next, creating a pathway in the synapse that, when traveled frequently enough, will become a default pathway between those two (or more) neurons. This is why 90 to 95 percent of our thoughts each day are the same as the day before.

Picture a mountain climber scaling the side of a mountain in which there is a 6-foot chasm. Though she's strapped in safely, when she gets to this tricky spot, her only options are to either quit and rappel down the mountain or take the risk and jump from one foothold and handhold to the next—across the chasm. She takes the leap, and once she's across she knows she'll be able to drive anchors, run a cable that she can hitch her safety harness to, and ride back and forth across the gap as often as she wants. In this visual the gap our mountain climber jumped is the synapse in the brain and the mountain climber herself is the electrical impulse that wants to move from one neuron to the next—the blue light that has to launch onto the unfamiliar ledge and establish the anchor for the cable.

For mountain climbers as well as for those of us creating new beliefs and neural pathways, establishing the anchor in unfamiliar territory that first time can feel difficult and dangerous. But each time we cross the divide, our confidence gets stronger and we can add more cables, which eventually makes that pathway along the divide strong enough to hold even more weight—to be even more reliable. From there we can branch out, more confidently building new bridges based on the strength of that first one, and we can feel safety in knowing that what we've created is a sturdy, reliable network of support. Once we've taken that first risk to jump to the new ledge of growth, repetition is what strengthens that bridge between neurons. Scientifically speaking, if we use the new bridge enough, it'll become the default pathway or belief, allowing our old beliefs to crumble.

Not long ago neurologists used to say the human brain became hardwired and couldn't achieve dramatic growth or changes past a certain age. This is no longer a commonly held belief. Today modern studies in neurobiology, specifically neuroplasticity—the flexibility of the brain over time and with use—proves the opposite. Sharon Begley, author of *Train Your Mind, Change Your Brain*, wrote that the brain retains the capability to change in response to experiences at any age. She found that it is even capable of altering its structure to the extent of creating new neurons and neuron paths. It is now common knowledge that it is possible for us to change our brain not only at 35—which I was when I began seriously working on myself—but even at 105! There's no such thing as unchangeable hardwiring of the brain.

Knowing that anything is possible when we understand that we can (and will) change our thoughts and our life gives us even *more* of a reason to undertake the rewriting of our subconscious programming. For most of us, 95 percent of our thoughts and actions come from our subconscious programming, which is often in conflict with the 5 percent from our conscious mind that contains our creativity, wishes, and desires. When the conscious and subconscious aren't working together toward the same goals, gaining momentum to improve our life feels like climbing a mountain without the proper gear: it won't be long before our exhaustion becomes greater than our drive to keep moving forward.

The goal is to have both the conscious and the subconscious parts of the mind working together, which can be done whether we're 8, 38, 88, or 108 years old.

So . . . do you want to change your brain and change your life?

As we talked about in Chapter 1, deliberately changing our focus is what helps shape that ever-present 5 percent of our conscious mind. Our focus changes what we see—whether it's a new opportunity, a favorite song on the radio, or a resolving of a tension or conflict. But remaining clear on our focus doesn't mean we can outrun that beast of our subconscious mind. Reconfiguring the other 95 percent of our programming in the subconscious mind is an ongoing and lifelong process that requires dedication and patience. What's fascinating is that despite this we will feel the effects almost immediately and there will be plenty to celebrate while we're working toward creating a new mind-set (or belief) to support our optimal joy. Often it takes a number of conscious pivots away from an old behavior before our brain will opt for the new pathway as the default . . . but it doesn't have to take long, and it *will* be worth it.

BUILDING A NEW MIND-SET

Picture this: You get a brand-new computer, fully loaded with software that promises to make your hectic life run more smoothly. Your eyes go wide when you start it up and see the desktop—every icon you wanted, and all in one place: your personal hard drive.

For the purposes of this metaphor, this computer is your brain, and the computer's hard drive is your subconscious programming. Just as each program on a computer can make it either run like a gazelle or crawl like a slug, each belief program in your brain either will guide you to act in ways that *connect* you to the life you most deeply desire or will act like corrupted software or firewalls to block and *disconnect* you from whatever it is you most want to have, be, do, or accomplish in your life.

In an ideal situation, each person's brain would come preprogrammed with beliefs that default to seeking out the experiences of optimal joy, love, accomplishment, and so on, but in the real world, we're born a blank slate. Our beliefs are not yet formed since they develop based on the primary influences of family, culture and community, and early childhood experiences.

As life happens we experience all sorts of things that can range from wonderful to tragic. And occasionally we might adopt a belief that tragic events follow us, or we deserve them, or some other version of that belief. When we believe a story that reinforces an emotional blockage, we're also reinforcing a neural pathway. Our beliefs become a barrier that holds us back from achieving our desires.

We adopt these barrier beliefs because we want to protect ourselves from some perceived threat; but keeping a barrier belief that is actively disconnecting us from possible joy in life is rarely intentional. In fact, I've yet to meet a single person, whether their childhood was idyllic or dysfunctional, whose barrier beliefs were put in place to *intentionally* keep them from having fun. As it turns out, the bulk of our programming—both conscious and subconscious—happens when we aren't actively seeking out what our programming is or could be.

In my case, while my childhood home life was challenging at times, my mom did much better for me than her mom did for her. I often told her that marrying my stepdad, Alex, was the best thing she ever did. He brought a grounded, steady demeanor to our home that Mom simply didn't have. Alex was raised by hard-working blue-collar parents who came from a different era. Their way of teaching Alex was through old-fashioned, strict morals and values, so he passed those morals and values down to me. He always had high expectations for my studies and lifestyle choices. However, throughout adolescence my interpretations of these expectations were often disconnected from his intentions, which led to harsh self-judgment.

The limiting beliefs I created as a child grew to be a whole system of limiting beliefs that shaped my choices and behaviors as an adult. It kept tripping me up, disconnecting me from my forward momentum and keeping me from achieving my goals. Over time I had to find a way to build a new mind-set so that I could be free from the ways that belief system held me back. Clearly, believing I was a loser didn't serve my creativity, my curiosity, or my goals, and I had to learn to change that.

OVERCOMING BARRIER BELIEFS

Despite the disempowering belief system of abandonment that I developed as a child, I got to where I am now through a combination of pure elbow grease, seeking guidance, a deep desire to feel good, and my inherent entrepreneurial spirit.

Even into adulthood on days when I was down on myself, it was easy to believe that I was inevitably destined for loneliness. Now that I'm in my 40s, I'm better equipped to rise above those early wired neural pathways. But in the beginning, it took a lot of practice, a lot of trial and error, to find a different way of seeing myself. I'm passing the shortcuts I've learned on to you, and these shortcuts have the ability to skyrocket your growth.

What stops a limiting or barrier belief right in its tracks? Taking action, regardless of how you feel about yourself. It seems simple enough, but let me explain.

Action will always be stronger than belief. There is more power in a single step forward than in the most firmly held conviction. In the past, whenever I heard phrases like *the power of now* or *be in the present moment*, I didn't get it. I didn't see how they applied to my life. But now I do. *The power of now* means deliberately making choices based on where you are today—not five or twenty-five years ago, and not from where you imagine you'll be six months from now. Staying focused in the here and now, and taking action from your present moment instead of sometime in the past or future, keeps you grounded and helps you move through your barrier beliefs.

Your power is *now*, and the heart of this power lies in where you choose to focus.

REPLACING YOUR BARRIER BELIEFS

Once we understand what our barrier beliefs are, we'll probably be ready to overcome them. Being willing to let go gives us the power to do it almost as soon as we see what it is we need to let go of. But as we know, nothing exists in a vacuum; so when we overcome a limiting belief, it's equally important to create a new belief—a new bridge between synapses—in its place.

How do we create new beliefs?

How do we know which beliefs need to be scrapped?

Without question, using Conscious Communications will create a new neural pathway, which will in turn create a new belief, and if you practice it enough, it'll become permanent. As the saying goes, *neurons that fire together, wire together.* If you're ready to change but are not sure where to start, pay attention to how you feel about certain topics like organized religion, romantic relationships, or money. Noticing your feelings in polarizing areas is a simple and easy way to begin reflecting on this.

Another way is to pay attention to what you obsess about. What excites you? Track these feelings too, and write them down. They'll help you see where you'd like to create a new pattern of beliefs.

EXERCISE: UNCOVERING YOUR BARRIER BELIEFS

This exercise is a quick way to help you begin to discover your barrier beliefs.

Rate how satisfied you are in each of the following areas of your life on a scale of 1 to 10 (10 being very satisfied):

- Health   _____

- Finances   _____

- Career   _____

- Relationships   _____

- Self-care   _____

- Spirituality   _____

For the areas you rated 5 or below, grab your journal and write down one or two things that are keeping you from having a higher number. What beliefs are behind the barriers you wrote down? Your answers will be a clue to what might be holding you back in that aspect of your life. For example, if my number for Spirituality is low, and I think about what is keeping that number from being higher, I might come to the conclusion that it stems from a fear of God, something I can trace back to a bad experience from my childhood. Or, perhaps my Relationships number is low. Maybe I frequently say things like, "All the good men are taken," or "Men these days are only interested in hookups."

I encourage you to look at your lowest area and ask yourself:

- What did my parents believe about this particular area?

- What is happening in this area of my life right now? What does it look like in this moment?

- How has my community impacted my current beliefs in this area?

- How do my current beliefs impact me and others?

- What would the ideal experience look like? (This is your opportunity to manifest! How do you *wish* things were? Write it out exactly as you dream it.)

Can you see how this exercise, and the thoughts you have uncovered, help to illuminate your beliefs?

As we've talked about, changing the conscious mind can be easier than we expect—we do that through redirecting our focus. The next frontier is lining up our subconscious programming with our creative, conscious mind so our subconscious and our conscious work together to connect us to the futures we desire.

Some examples of people who've done this important work are a few notable public figures such as Oprah Winfrey, J. K. Rowling, Jim Carrey, and Maya Angelou. Each of them overcame the perceived obstacles of their early programming so they could achieve their goals. Oprah Winfrey is often quoted as saying that "a person can change his future by merely changing his attitude." Oprah is so successful because she *believes* she can be, despite the horrors that befell her as a youth, and she's found the backdoor approach to achieving her ultimate goals. These people, along with many others, learned that the more emotional a decision is, the stronger the drive is to achieve the intended outcome. They also understand that, on the other side of that coin, when you can detach unwanted emotions from a memory or a decision, the world around you becomes easier to navigate, your peace levels increase, and the distance between you and your dreams gets shorter and shorter.

STAND TALL

When you change your internal beliefs to align with your conscious desires, you will begin to value yourself more. Seeing your value will guide you to raise your standards and be open to even more opportunities and experiences, which will create new neural pathways. This circles back to the lens of your perception being either smudged or clear. Identifying that you're experiencing your life through the lens of misperception is in itself a synchronicity, but being able to clean off that avidya and see your life through a clear lens is the real magic.

When you carry yourself throughout your days with the confidence of seeing the truth of yourself and the world around you, the probabilities of events in your life will dramatically change. Even standing taller in line at the grocery store will create a different impression on people than if you stood hunched over. You can—and deserve to—stand tall.

I'd like to show you one way to clear the misperception from the way you see yourself and your life. I've done it, and I have reaped tremendous benefits from it. I'm confident you will too.

100 THINGS I LOVE ABOUT ME

Relationship coach and author Dave Elliott helps his clients (predominately women) begin to identify, appreciate, and embrace all the qualities about themselves that they had previously ignored or suppressed. Dave assigned me an activity to write out a list of 100 things I loved about myself. It struck me as a valuable exercise, so I began working on it right away.

Because of how much I've trained myself through physical exercise, breath work and meditation, and reprogramming old beliefs, I wasn't surprised at how quickly I was able to write out the more immediately obvious qualities I loved about myself. However, I *was* surprised that I still had more than half my list to go when I came to the place where I had to really think about what to write down next.

I had to exercise patience and self-compassion as I sat with my unfinished list, in that empty space between ideas, as I waited for another item to occur to me. I saw tremendous value even in the process of sitting with the unfinished list and trusting that another idea would come—trusting that there was plenty more for me to love about myself.

I remember the day I realized what the last two items on my list were. I sketched them into my journal as numbers 99 and 100: *I am a radiant woman* and *I am a powerful creator*, I wrote. I felt such relief when I met my target!

A strange thing happened within 24 hours of finishing the list. All of a sudden, friends, acquaintances, and complete strangers started coming up to me with out-of-the-blue compliments that aligned perfectly with the essence of who I am and what I'd identified as the last two things that I loved about myself: that I am radiant, and that I am a powerful creator. Had I not pushed through the resistance, I'd have never gotten to the last two qualities, which I now see as two of my most prized assets.

What I found by finally letting go of my past disempowering stories was that I had created an empty space that I could now fill with new triumphant stories and forward momentum. Finding my value served to increase my "worthiness quotient," and once I understood my value I could consciously create from a place of empowerment.

I want that for you too.

EXERCISE: YOUR 100 THINGS

Just as the exercise at the end of Chapter 1 helps you refocus your conscious mind toward an attitude of gratitude, helping you to recognize that which is beautiful in your life, this exercise will help you uncover the deeper parts of yourself that you appreciate so you can both get to know yourself better and know your true value.

Open to a blank sheet of paper in your journal.

Title the page, "My 100 Things List."

Begin writing down one thing at a time that you love about yourself. (If you struggle with the word *love*, you can substitute *like* or *accept*.)

There is no right or wrong way to do this, and no quality—whether superficial or microscopic or even invisible—is exempt from the list if you identify it as something you love about yourself.

Know these truths:

1. **Everyone experiences resistance.** It'll probably take you more than 24 hours to write out your list; it took me four weeks to finish mine!

2. **Put silly things on the list.** We often find ourselves far down the totem pole of priorities with regard to our families, our kids, and even our work life. Because of this it's not only common but it's expected that you'll hit a blank wall and want to say, *That's it; that's all I love about myself,* without hitting 100. Do you love the fact that you can still feel beautiful wearing sweatpants and no makeup? Or do you love that you're more into documentaries than regular TV? Or that you pay your bills on time? Don't put restrictions on what you list as things you love about yourself.

3. **Sweat through it.** There is a method to this madness, so if you find yourself feeling great resistance, know this is your subconscious programming (remember, that's 95 percent of your beliefs!) trying to get you to fall back in line. Don't give up. Be willing to write

down the littlest thing that you love about yourself. And remember to add things here and there as they come to you throughout the day (because they will).

4. **Spend time with your list.** If you're feeling really ambitious, set aside time each morning in the same way you might for writing a birthday or thank-you card you have to put in the mail that day. Even if you only come up with one thing a day, you'll feel the positive momentum building in your consciousness. And when you do eventually write your 100th quality, let yourself rejoice in your persistence and also in your faith that you have so much to give the world.

In the next chapter, we'll dive deeper into understanding how the nervous system, despite its best intentions, isn't always very helpful. So far we've only laid the foundation for growing. And we need this foundation, because when life turns upside down (as it is known to do), our emotional state triggers chemical chain reactions in our brain and nervous system. If we can learn to manage or mitigate the intensity of the cascading chemicals, we can see even more clearly just how important it is that we've embarked on this journey . . . and how at the center of it all, whatever we blurt out from our mouths will either connect us with or disconnect us from our personal path of transformation.

CHAPTER 3

YOUR NERVOUS SYSTEM: FRIEND OR FRENEMY?

"Happiness is when what you think, what you say,
and what you do are in harmony."

— ATTRIBUTED TO MAHATMA GANDHI

In this chapter we will discuss the importance of the nervous system and how it's designed to help us during times of stress and to survive life-or-death situations. We will also learn how to manage toxic buildup, tap into our mind-body connection, and move up the frequency scale of emotion.

POWERING YOUR CHEMISTRY

One day when I was in my late teens, my grandpa told me a story that I'll never forget. Years earlier, my uncle had just returned home from a ride on his Harley when he lost his footing and fell backward, accidentally pulling the 800-pound machine down on top of himself. My petite aunt heard the crash from upstairs and raced down to the garage to find her husband pinned beneath and being crushed by nearly half a ton of metal. Her instincts kicked in, and without missing a beat, in a rush of superhuman strength, she lifted the bike off my uncle and saved his life.

How did she do that?

First, when my aunt heard the crash, she went from a relaxed state to being on high alert, a shift that activated her sympathetic nervous system, which is responsible for the *fight-or-flight* response. By the time she got down to the garage and was on full-fledged high alert, her brain produced the right chemical recipe to give her the superhuman strength we usually only see in superhero movies or hear about in noteworthy stories of heroism.

Second, the threat my aunt faced was real; when her brain initiated the fight-or-flight trigger, she had the opportunity to *actually use* the chemicals her brain had pushed out from her nervous system and into her body. Because of a chemical recipe her brain produced at the sense of possible danger, she lifted a solid machine that was eight times her weight right off of her husband without giving it a second thought.

Our body really is designed to handle intense and highly stressful situations; it gives us a dose of the chemicals we need to handle dangerous encounters, and then it restores us to our natural, prestress state. But it's a delicate balance between fight-or-flight and rest-and-digest.

Without going into too much detail, let's get into the science of how this works and why it matters.

THE DYSFUNCTIONAL FREAK-OUT

Whenever you experience a life-threatening situation like my aunt did, your hypothalamus (a tiny region in the base of your brain) rings an alarm. That alarm sends the memo to your adrenals to release a surge of hormones, adrenaline and cortisol being the usual leaders of the pack, to help you manage the threat, whether it's real or perceived.

The most fascinating part of the fight-or-flight system is that it cannot determine whether a threat is real or perceived. For example, any time you've heard a loud engine backfire, watched a horror movie, or even had a terrible nightmare, your fear of what you think is going to happen will trigger the sympathetic nervous system. It doesn't matter if the thing that startled you is a threat to your life or not. Just like a soldier, the brain takes orders from the mind based on what you experience—whether pleasant or unpleasant—and sends a message to your adrenals to make sure they create chemical recipes that match the experience you are having, or the experience you *think* you are having.

In the triggered fight-or-flight mode, the sympathetic nervous system is engaged. This mode happens more often now than say, 200 years ago, simply because of the intensity of our busy society. We're constantly fielding a barrage of infiltrations of our nervous system in the form of phones ringing, e-mail pings demanding our immediate response, kids' urgent requests, sirens, et cetera. The nervous system registers all these triggers and identifies most of them as threats . . . whether they are or not. When you perceive a threat, all your energy and chemicals are redirected to the muscles whose job is to keep you alive. Their function—*survival at all costs*—will keep you alive, but as a result less energy and chemicals are directed to the growth and regeneration of cells.

Imagine living in the wild, and suddenly you realize you're being chased by a lion. In this situation your life depends on whether or not you can escape the hungry cat. The stress hormone recipe your body creates is designed to give you ultimate, superhuman strength to escape, and that response comes from the primitive parts of your brain that are wired for survival.

In today's modernized culture, the things we perceive as threats—a meeting with an angry boss, an embarrassing situation, et cetera—don't require that dramatic surge of chemicals to help us escape certain death. But our body launches into fight-or-flight mode anyway because our brain can't tell the difference. The high number of times our body launches into fight-or-flight—and how commonplace it is for us to get stuck there—is now at a critical point in human history.

Why?

In the wild we'd run away from the lion (or die trying), thereby using up the chemicals our body just created for the purpose of survival. However, when there is no lion, and the perceived threat is based in our mind and not in real-world danger, we don't burn through the chemicals. The bad news is that when we don't get rid of those excess chemicals, they stay in the body and become toxic.

Toxic levels of stress hormones are what we call *chronic elevated stress,* and it's directly linked to other chronic conditions such as cardiovascular disease, a weak immune system, dysregulated metabolism, and increased agitation or irritability, according to the American Psychological Association. These elevated levels of stress also impair our emotional well-being and our central nervous systems. When we're in fight-or-flight for extended periods of time, it's not just our physical health that is compromised; chronic elevated stress also shuts down learning, creativity, and cognition, which isn't a good combination for our overall health. Forget about ingenuity or abstract thinking when we're feeling that kind of emotional trigger.

The yin to the above yang is how the parasympathetic nervous system works. Simply put, the parasympathetic system promotes growth and regeneration. Our body sloughs off an immeasurable volume of cells each day, and this part of our nervous system is what helps us regrow and regenerate cells. But it can't do any of that if fight-or-flight is regularly kicked into high gear and never takes a break from the race.

In light of this, can you see how important it is to get rid of the overabundance of stress hormones in your body so your parasympathetic nervous system can have its turn to do its thing? The parasympathetic and the sympathetic nervous systems cooperate to keep the whole of you balanced, healthy, and alive, but they're really in competition with each other. What that means is that while you're in fight-or-flight mode, your parasympathetic nervous system is off, unable to provide support to your internal organs. Between the sympathetic nervous system (fight-or-flight) and the parasympathetic (rest-and-digest), the sympathetic always wins. Because, really, when you're being chased by a lion, cell regrowth, hormone balancing, and proper organ function take a no-questions-asked back seat to the priority of outrunning a Jurassic-sized cat for your survival. Once you realize that the threat is not real or that it is no longer a threat, the parasympathetic system kicks in and returns your body to a natural, prestress state.

So when you *feel* and *act* like you're being chased by a lion, even though you're at work at your desk all day, your body doesn't know the difference. It still prioritizes survival over other standard functions, or over creative thinking, for example. It wants to keep you alive, and it'll do everything in its power to help you escape that lion—even if the "lion" is really your boss, a call from the principal at your child's school, or a hellacious level-10 argument.

MANAGING THE TOXIC BUILDUP

The nervous system processes your experiences and sends a rush of powerful hormones into your body to produce whatever recipe is necessary to match your experience. Later in the chapter, we'll talk about how body movement affects your chemistry and how you can use your chemistry to positively affect your body.

For now, in light of knowing that your nervous system is giving orders to your body, here are tips that I think will help you keep your nervous system balanced:

1. **Exercise.** Take the time to get the chemicals out of your body through physical activity. Some forms of exercise, like running, burn off the stress hormones, which is absolutely necessary, while others, like yoga, stimulate the parasympathetic nervous system, promoting growth, healing, and regeneration.

2. **Control your sensory input.** Avoid exposing yourself to stressful, violent television, high-stress physical environments, and any experience that creates tension in one of your sensory areas, meaning what you see, hear, feel, smell, and taste.

3. **Do things to stimulate the parasympathetic nervous system.** Adopt a relaxation practice. Perhaps consciously measure your breathing. Or lightly rub your bottom lip from one side to the other and back with your finger, which awakens those nerve endings, quickening the body's restoration to a pre-stress state.

4. **Avoid talking on your cell phone on the drive home.** You know that the person you call is going to bitch about their day, and someone who's been waiting for you to get off work so they can unload is not the best person to talk to. Give yourself some transition time between work and home.

5. **Surround yourself with positivity.** Listen to an uplifting story or audiobook, or read something pleasing to you.

6. **Properly nourish your body.** Drink plenty of water and eat foods that keep your mood balanced, as opposed to food or drink that is likely to cause a spike in either direction (like sugar or excess alcohol).

7. **Get a full night's sleep.** The average person needs seven to eight hours of sleep each night, and sleep is very important to your health and healing.

8. **Adopt a vitamin regimen.** Take supplements to help encourage the body's natural production of serotonin or dopamine, like ginkgo biloba or curcumin.

9. **Do your research.** But don't self-diagnose or guess at supplementation. Don't hesitate to get help from a naturopath.

CHEMICAL RECIPES AND FIFTY
SHADES OF CHOCOLATE CAKE

When I'm teaching my workshops, I'll sometimes talk about chocolate cake. I'll rattle off all the types of chocolate cake I can think of in the moment: red velvet cake, hot fudge cake, chocolate lava cake, white chocolate cake, flourless chocolate cake, German chocolate cake . . . I won't go on, but you can imagine just how many different types of chocolate cakes there are. Along with making my participants hungry, I also make them think: As many different types of chocolate cake as there are, each one has *hundreds* of recipes that will all produce a version of that type of chocolate cake. What kind of chemical recipe do you want in your body?

In the same way that a chocolate cake's recipe determines its texture and flavor, each emotion you have is determined by a chemical recipe in your body. The way the nervous system reacts to a certain experience generates a message for your adrenal glands, which will then create and send out the perfect chemical recipe to your body to match the emotion associated with that experience (or memory of the experience).

Consider the emotion of sadness. It's a simple enough concept at first glance, but in actuality there is an entire spectrum of degrees and varieties of sadness. You could be feeling weepy and blue, experiencing tidal waves of tears, or feel like you are walking on shattered glass—but all of it can be categorized as sadness. Though the ingredients to create the varying types of sadness are mostly the same, each variety of emotion on the sadness spectrum is created by a specific chemical recipe. Imagine you turn on the radio and hear a song that connects you to a sad moment in your life. When that happens the brain runs the program connected to that memory, and the body goes straight to the emotional state you were in when you first experienced the triggering event by re-creating the same chemical recipe. How profound the sadness is in that moment is related to how much we've grown and either strengthened or loosened our grip on our past.

Just as constant stress produces an overabundance of stress hormones that remain stuck in our body, when we experience persistent states of emotional strain, those chemicals can get stuck in overdrive in our body too. Have you ever had someone impatiently snap at you and then justify their reaction as, "This is just the way I am"? In a way this is true . . . but only temporarily. Any emotional state that is triggered and long-lasting creates a more solid neural pathway that makes it easier to default to that emotional state. The good news is it's neither permanent nor irreversible.

Just like scientists used to believe our brain was hardwired by the time we reached a certain age, at one point brain researchers also thought that the genetic blueprint we were born with was unchangeable, and that that blueprint would drive certain distinguishing features about us, like hair color, height, or the strength of our vision. That's no longer the case. Today there's an entire specialty within the study of genetics—*epi*genetics—that understands that our body can turn genes on and off based on our environment. We have much more influence on the outcome of our genetics than we previously believed.

This means, for instance, that when we're in a toxic environment we are activating certain genes and affecting the way they express themselves in our body, and deactivating, or turning *off,* other genes. Over time our environment changes the way our genes show up in our body. We can suppress the best expression of our genes by prolonged exposure to high stress, emotional duress, or toxicity. And we can also change them with exposure to laughter. During a talk given by author and speaker Joe Dispenza, I learned that simply laughing for long periods of time can influence the way our genes express themselves in our body. In his book *Breaking the Habit of Being Yourself,* Dispenza explains that test subjects with type 2 diabetes watched a comedy show for one hour, and 23 different gene expressions were altered just by that hour spent laughing. So the feeling of letting laughter take over your body is only one of the many benefits a 60-minute laugh fest will have on you in the long term.

Norman Cousins, author, professor, activist, and colleague of Albert Einstein, gives us another example. When he was 39 years old, Cousins was diagnosed with heart disease. Having researched and taught extensively on the biochemistry of human emotions at the school of medicine at University of California, Los Angeles, Cousins believed that the key to healing and fighting illness was in our beliefs. To treat his illness, he trained himself to laugh for sustained periods of time. And as a result of his laughter, he was healed of heart disease to the extent that it was no longer life-threatening. Doctors were shocked at his recovery, but Cousins was graciously vindicated, since this was the outcome he had expected. Using laughter as one of his primary means of self-healing, Cousins died at 75 years old—36 years after his fatal heart-disease diagnosis. This is the kind of power our thoughts have over our physiology.

The way we control and influence our gene expression is by the choices we make in our everyday life. The healthier our choices, the healthier our life. This is the fundamental basis of emotional health, and gene expression is one of the ways our emotions directly affect our physiology.

We talked about the recipes for sadness, but there are just as many varieties of feel-good chemical recipes in our body. Let's take falling in love as an example. It's more than likely that at one point or another all of us have fallen in love. We all probably know that euphoric feeling that seems to wash over everything in our life when we're newly in love—like everything is dipped in Love Potion Number 9. When we're in this state, we're producing a chemical recipe of serotonin, dopamine, oxytocin, and vasopressin—all chemicals that are designed to make us feel good.

There are a multitude of combinations of happy hormones in your body, like endorphins, phenylethylamine, and ghrelin, all of which can contribute to the chemical recipe of feeling good. But the point is this: you need to get familiar with how to increase these chemicals. You're making strides in the direction of controlling the chemical recipes in your body, and as you do, you're going to be getting more acquainted with these ingredients. These happy hormones are your friends—and they would love to get to know you on the BFF level. (And I'm sure the feeling is mutual.)

IF HAPPINESS WERE A CHOICE, WOULDN'T WE BE HAPPY ALL THE TIME!

In researching the nervous system, I have found that the thalamus and the pituitary are the master glands that are in charge of every other chemical output in the body.

If you've damaged the thalamus, it is nearly impossible to regulate hormones in your body, and that makes it difficult to make happy hormones. If you're stuck in that unhappy place for an extended amount of time—perhaps many years—it *will* become your personality. Through years of these chemicals being put out and the neural pathways getting reinforced to support the chemistry, you're strengthening your programming, your beliefs, your 60,000 thoughts a day, and your conscious and subconscious to make your unhappy statements feel true.

Whenever I hear people use phrases like *happiness is a choice* or *sadness is a choice*, I wince, because I don't believe it to be that simple. Instead I'd say that happiness is a set of chemicals and sadness is a set of chemicals, and all emotions affect our mind, as well as our physiology. We do have some control over those feelings, but it takes knowledge and effort to change those chemicals.

A person who can simply *choose* to be happy is an obvious example of someone whose baseline is happy to begin with. The rest of the population, who have a way to go before happiness is their default, have to make a choice each day (and sometimes from moment to moment) in a different direction to dig out of what feels like a deep grave. The closer you are to sadness or despair, the harder it becomes to climb out. This is because when you're feeling despair, it's not just *one* thing that feels hopeless— you likely feel despair because many elements of your life have been affected by hopelessness. All it takes to move out of despair is one different thought that feels even a fraction better than despair and you can begin to change your chemistry. It's hard to just "choose" a positive thought, so my experience is based in action. You can choose to watch a kitten video, force yourself to read from or add something to your 100 Things list, or take a bath. It doesn't matter what it is; one small action in a direction that will ultimately heal you can change everything. It all begins with what you are focused on right in this moment.

SEEING YOUR SITUATION FOR WHAT IT IS

Your perception, your beliefs, and your focus create everything in your life. A certain negative belief about love or money, for example, will alert the brain to send a message to your adrenals to create a chemical recipe to match the feeling to the belief, which will ultimately disconnect you from experiencing love or abundance. It's human nature to slip and fall into, say, "abandonment soup" or "poverty mind-set soup" on occasion. But swimming in that soup is another thing altogether. In fact, the way you see your situation—your perception of it—determines your experience. For example, if a friend hasn't called you back after a few days, do you slip into a belief that you're being abandoned? Or if you have an unexpected expense, do you default to a belief that you're destined for the poorhouse? Or are you instead able to see these experiences through a lens of correct perception and not personalize them? It's from this place of perception that you make choices, and these choices shape the direction of your life.

When we get lodged in a belief about ourselves or the world around us that is not true, we're living in a chemical recipe based on a misperception—that avidya I talked about in Chapter 2. The cleaner our lens of perception, the cleaner our chemicals. Unpleasant feelings are a way for our body to communicate to us. But we've gotten to a point in society where listening to the body isn't encouraged, so we ignore the connection between feelings and our body. Because of this, we don't connect the biological impulse associated with discomfort with the possibility that maybe—*just* maybe—we're being signaled to make a change in our life or our circumstances.

About a year ago, I witnessed my own personal combination of chemicals that were triggered by a breakup, and the experience helped me heal in a more integrated, fully embodied way. My then-boyfriend sat across the table and explained plainly to me that he couldn't see me anymore, and that he wanted us to "detach" from each other. I was heartbroken.

That night I lay in my bed, crying and sobbing uncontrollably. After a good ten minutes of this, I blinked my eyes hard and wiped the tears away . . . I realized I had been running a subconscious program that had everything to do with being abandoned at four years old and nothing to do with this breakup. In that moment—where just seconds before, I was sobbing over breaking up with my boyfriend—I connected this truth for myself, and suddenly I felt lighter.

I drew in a deep breath and pulled the covers up to my chin, thinking more. The reality was that I was just as much a part of the decision not to see him anymore as he was. No one was abandoning me. Understanding this was like flipping a switch. I realized that as soon as I had triggered the program of abandonment from when I felt abandoned and helpless at four years old, everything in my body ignited the chemical recipe of abandonment from that first original wound.

Instantly, I reviewed every breakup I'd ever gone through since high school, and I saw a pattern. Any time I experienced a breakup, I drowned in what felt like debilitating depression that was so bad there were stretches of time when I wasn't a functioning adult. As I looked closer at this pattern, it was also clear that I typically stayed in that state until something broke the cycle, like a vacation or a new boyfriend. And every one of those depressions was a re-creation of the emotional state of that four-year-old child who felt like her life would be at risk if she were left alone.

The moment I realized this, I sat up in bed and said out loud to myself, "Don't run that program. You don't have to do this to yourself, and you don't have to spiral into depression." I stopped crying. And I noticed that when I stopped the program from running full steam ahead, I went from feeling desperation to anxiousness, then to mild sadness. As I drifted into the theta waves right before I fell asleep, I thought about how fascinating it was to discover, from the inside, what it felt like to stop an unwanted program from diving into a chemical recipe cycle that would have normally knocked me sideways out of the momentum of my life.

I slept on the possibility that I had experienced a shift in my consciousness, and when I woke up the next day, I wasn't depressed. In fact, it was more than not being depressed; I was actually happy. I got out of bed and went about my morning, noticing the newness of what it felt like to be the captain of my own emotional ship. It was liberating. I sat down to write in my journal, which gave me an outlet for the happiness I was feeling. As I started writing, I got more and more excited, and as I got more excited, that fueled even more excitement.

To clarify, this isn't to say that I didn't feel occasional waves of sadness over the breakup; I did. The difference is that I could finally see the situation for what it was and what it wasn't, and I didn't fall prey to an old abandonment program that didn't serve my needs anymore.

THE FREQUENCY SCALE

Just as we discussed with the spectrum of sadness, there is a spectrum that contains all emotions, which I refer to as the "frequency scale." I talk about moving up or down the frequency scale. Sure there is happiness, but there's an entire *spectrum* of happiness. Say the frequency scale is 0–100, with 0 being complete and absolute rock-bottom despair and 100 being pure bliss. When we're stuck in an unwanted feeling on the frequency scale—despair, for example—we can't jump from despair to ecstasy in one fell swoop. Like moving up a spiral staircase, we go a step (or two) at a time, from despair to anger to frustration to irritation, and so forth, until we get to a neutral place.

When I had my aha moment about stopping my abandonment program from taking me offline after that breakup, you saw that I went from despairing to anxious to sad. I moved up the frequency scale a little at a time. By morning I had gotten my mojo back; I actually felt happy. But I couldn't have jumped straight from despair to happiness; that's not how the frequency scale of emotions works. It takes time for our body to cook up a new chemical recipe.

Additionally, when we are at the bottom of the frequency scale, we are seeing everything through a lens of misperception. What we see is filtered through our mud-covered glasses, and disengaging from that mud can be sticky. Once we've lived in fight-or-flight for a long time, being constantly edgy and overreactive, it doesn't take much to trigger despair and keep us circling the drain of that point on the frequency scale.

LISTENING INWARD

From the moment we are born, our tiny infant body uses our five senses to process every bit of information to which we are exposed. As we grow we naturally develop programs that help us navigate our life: programs that are based on our experiences and our perception of our experiences. In addition to the programs we develop, there are a number of other basic human programs we are born with—*primal* programs—that function to keep us alive.

From birth onward, our body calculates each new encounter or experience based on all the other information we've ever learned and experienced, and it does this at hyperspeed, faster than our conscious mind can understand. This processing ability is a perfect example of our inexplicable prefab instincts for survival, and for how (and why) we can even make split-second decisions in the first place. If, for example, you were attacked by a dog when you were a kid, any time you encounter a dog in your environment, your body will calculate the risk of another dog attack. Chances are, without conscious thought, you'll find a way to avoid the dog.

Have you ever had a feeling about something that you couldn't help but describe as a "gut" feeling? The idea that we have gut feelings has been around forever, but it wasn't until recently that we've been able to understand exactly what it means when we have one of these experiences.

In 2007 social scientist Malcolm Gladwell published a book entitled *Blink: The Power of Thinking without Thinking*. In it he studies case after case of real-life situations where people—ranging from mobster gamblers to professional athletes to museum curators—were faced with a decision. He then tracks their instinctual, immediate judgment of the situation, and charts how that initial assessment lined up with whatever big-picture decision they ended up making.

Throughout the book Gladwell charts the concept of *thin-slicing*, which is a term that refers to the action of making a quick assessment of someone or something, without a full explanation of the situation. These quick responses or judgments turn out to be similar to the responses or reactions of others whose assessment is based on even more information. But the kicker with thin-slicing is that decisions made according to gut feelings are even more accurate than the decisions people make when given the full picture and asked to use logic.

Why is that?

We now know what we've always known: the body doesn't lie. In addition to having a body that processes experiences and exposures, we also have thinking cells spread throughout the body. You'd be right to imagine from this that we have thinking cells in our skin. But we most notably also have those thinking cells in our gut. Yes, you read that right: you have brain cells in your belly. In fact, there are more than 100 million nerve cells lining your gastrointestinal tract, all the way from your esophagus to your rectum. In his 2011 study, gastroenterologist and UCLA professor Dr. Emeran Mayer stated that the gut-brain connection likely affects motivation, higher cognitive functions, and intuitive decision making. These thinking cells all have access to the master file system in the brain, and faster than any of our other functions, our body calculates what's before us and sends that information back to the brain to help us identify those gut feelings.

Often we are somehow discouraged from listening to the calculations our body makes and sends to our brain. It makes sense that, since we live in a reason-driven society, when we can't articulate a reason to support our gut feelings, we too often ignore them. What's more, when we have a deep desire that conflicts with the calculation our body gave us, we can easily override our initial feeling or instinct about something, but we often regret it.

Consider something as simple as having an aversion to a certain food, and later finding out you have an allergy to it. These reactions aren't cognitive functions, but they're certainly not made without thinking.

Other ways our body relays information to our mind is through our senses of smell, sight (including reading body language), sound, and touch. When we're "smelling danger," we're using what's otherwise known as the olfactory glands, but our body is also calculating billions of bits of information through what we see, touch, and hear too. Despite being human, we still make choices about one another by using these more primal senses over our logic—and it's to our benefit. Whenever you've heard the saying that *dogs can smell fear,* what we're really saying is that the chemical recipe that makes up the hormones associated with fear, along with the body language of fear, is noticeable to animals. Though human receptors are different, our senses really do give us insight as to what's going on with the people around us.

FAKING IT UNTIL MAKING IT

During my divorce it was clear to me that exercise was the only activity I could do that would make both my mind and body feel better at the same time. I regularly went to kickboxing classes at my gym to help dislodge the stress hormones I built up every day. But each time I walked by the yoga room on my way to the showers, I dismissed it with judgment, believing yoga was boring and "not for me."

Six years went by before I decided to give yoga a try. It did bore me to tears at first, especially since in the silent space of the yoga room, my head was still filled with stressful chatter about my divorce. Once the movement began to loosen the traumas in my body, something clicked. I began going to yoga with a journal to write down my insights, and through yoga my suppressed emotions started rising up to the surface, like little effervescent champagne bubbles. Sometimes it would trigger a rush of tears and emotions—feelings that came from deep within my body and that my conscious mind hadn't thought of. Nine out of ten times, I didn't even know why I was crying.

What I know now is that the emotions of our traumas stay in our body, especially when we don't actively work to release them or when those recipes have several decades of buildup in our tissues. Yoga is one way we can dislodge the stored emotions from our cells. In essence yoga is the body telling the mind what to do, instead of the other way around, reciprocally completing the mind-body feedback loop.

Another aspect that feeds into the mind-body connection is body language. If you slump as you sit at your desk, your body receives the message that you're feeling down, and you'll produce the necessary chemicals to create the feeling that matches the physical form you're in. The same is true for what is now known as a "power pose." In a study conducted by Amy Cuddy, participants were asked to do two high-level power poses for two minutes each. This consisted of sitting with their feet on the desk and their hands behind their head, then standing and leaning on their hands against a desk. Samples were taken of the participants' saliva, and these showed that levels of cortisol (the stress hormone) decreased by 25 percent and testosterone levels increased by 19 percent for both men and women after they did the power poses. Other exercises such as standing like a superhero or holding a pencil horizontally between your teeth (which forces your cheeks to adopt a smile) for two solid minutes are also ways to increase your endorphins to make you feel happier. Your body is telling your mind what to do.

The better the body is running, the better you'll hear the body's messages. The most magical aspect of body language is that it is communicating back to the nervous system, completing the feedback loop, and actually affecting the chemicals in your brain.

While body language is a great way to get yourself hyped up, another way to do it is through words. The words you choose on a regular basis are extremely powerful. Your words broadcast not only to your cells but also to your environment, which affects your identity, how people see you, and how they treat you, which loops back in to how you identify, see, and treat yourself. This is one of the most direct ways that you move yourself, and others around you, up and down the frequency scale.

If you seek to more accurately process your environment and make better choices, one of the most direct ways to do that is by keeping your vessel clean. This doesn't only relate to eating well or exercising, although yoga will help align the mind and the body, and this improved focus can help us make better choices. Keeping your vessel clean means being aware of as much of your body as you can be.

It always comes back to the nervous system. Ask yourself, *Am I conscious of the ways I can influence my own chemical recipe? Or even the ways I can make sure I have healthy chemical makers?* What are you doing to support the systems in your body that create vitality?

Even clutter in your house affects your vessel. Feeding your mind with ideas that strengthen your focus and staying away from toxic people or toxic input are other ways to support your vitality. Whether it's your health, finances, career, relationships, self-care, or spirituality, it's all connected. Like driving a car with a flat tire, having one area of your life out of balance will only let you get so far.

GETTING ALL YOUR NEURONS IN A ROW

If you were to address only one area of your life—your focus, your beliefs, or your chemical recipes—it'd be true to say that your life would change. But because more is possible for you, we're going to be addressing all three. When you consider dialing your control in over all three, that's when you get the surge of power to know that anything is possible. Once you get these three components in alignment, you'll be so powerful that you'll be able to move mountains, and you will experience an *explosion* of synchronicities. Although it'd be hard to count, I'd venture to bet they'll explode exponentially.

Why is that?

For starters, when you start listening to your body, to those gut feelings, you'll make the decision to call that person, make that right turn, or spend that extra five minutes on the phone with your sibling . . . which will lead the way to the types of synchronicities that will blow your mind. Just seeing how things line up for you will help you create new beliefs, generate a deeper connection in the action center in your brain, and train you to notice that *you're actually feeling great.*

When your chemical recipe is dialed in to happiness, it becomes the jazz that juices everything else up in your life. Harnessing the trio of choosing your focus, reprogramming beliefs, and managing your chemical recipes—this is the spark for true transformation.

Have you ever had a day when you felt like you had the Midas touch? When it seemed that everything you encountered turned to gold? Did that make you feel happy? What hormones were being created that day? The truth is, when you are happy, the chemical recipe that's swirling around in your body inspires you to take leaps of faith, speak kind words, and feel generally fantastic, all of which creates more opportunities for change.

When you feel this good, it seems that things will continue to go well for you, and the way to keep that train on its tracks is through consciously harnessing the power you have over the three prongs of change: focus, beliefs, and chemistry. All those happy hormones you've been encountering, like dopamine, endorphins, phenylethylamine, and ghrelin, can become, with some effort and consistent focus, the baseline for your new normal.

The whole reason we need to control the chemicals in our body is because when we do so, we feel good. And when we feel good, we're in a better place to make good choices. And making good choices makes us feel good, which is that feedback loop of happiness we're going for. When we experience the optimal chemical recipe in our body for happiness, those better choices will become the norm and we'll experience *vidya* ("wisdom"), which is the opposite of avidya ("misperceiving"), with more regularity. Being in this state allows us to scan our lives through a cleaner lens and make measured decisions without feeling stuck with anything less than our highest good.

Have you ever noticed that when you fall in love, everything else in your life seems to pop with good news, including things in the life of your new significant other? This is because being in love creates a brain-flooding chemical recipe that feels amazing, and when you feel that good, you naturally go up on the frequency scale of emotion. And going up that scale has a ripple effect, in that the people around you start to seem happier too. And when everyone in your immediate vicinity is higher on that frequency scale of emotions, you'll attract all sorts of other kinds of magic into your life!

So how do you get to this happy state?

Step 1: Train your focus. Remember that what you focus on grows, and that the easiest way to train your focus is through a daily practice of declaring gratitude.

Step 2: Stop retelling stories from your past that don't serve you. This helps in loosening your grip on those stories, which will then give you space to tell better-feeling stories.

Step 3: Get control of the chemical recipes in your body. Knowing that intense responses are triggered by historical events in our life, we can redirect our focus in order to create new (and better-feeling) chemical recipes.

Whenever you hear people say, "You have to do the work," know that *this* is what it looks like when you're doing the work. You're loosening your grip and attachment to how things were, letting go of old, worn-out stories that don't work for you anymore, and putting the body and mind in connection with one another so they can work together *for* you instead of against you.

Whether you have big dreams or simply want to have a better self-image, in order to change, you must have a firm foundation. This is the elixir that will fast-track you to a life that feels better than you could ever have imagined.

This is your foundation. To take that foundation metaphor a little further, think about the foundations of your house. They need to be checked on periodically, right? A house that isn't maintained will eventually fall apart. Your nervous system requires maintenance too, or it too will deteriorate. The following exercise will provide suggestions for the upkeep of your nervous system.

EXERCISE: ZEN 10

This is a list of 10 ways to support your nervous system, and they all do essentially the same thing. Each will reduce your stress, provide an overall increase in happiness, and help with issues in the tissues, targeting the neurons and chemicals in your brain and getting them to work for you. You're going to pick three: one that you will commit to doing every day, one that you will commit to doing once a week, and one that you will commit to doing once a month.

Some of them may resonate with you more than others—many of us wince at the idea of meditation, while others can't wait to get to the gym. So as you go through the list, choose carefully, and use the following criteria:

- Does this feel like self-care? Is this something you'll look forward to, something that will feel like a gift you give yourself?

- Is this something you can realistically stick with?

- Can you commit to doing this once a day, once a week, once a month?

1. **Yoga.** Many people underestimate the power of yoga, and how a little goes a very long way. If you invest even 15 to 20 minutes a day, you will receive a huge return on your investment. Yoga strengthens your immune system and it lowers your heart rate and blood pressure. It stimulates the parasympathetic nervous system, which is the powerhouse of relaxation. And yoga doesn't have to be hard—it's not all "power yoga." Restorative yoga practices like yin yoga or yoga nidra directly

stimulate the vagus nerve, regulating your heart rate, bringing your body peace.

2. Meditation. Meditation is the secret fountain of youth. It causes natural increases of DHEA, GABA, endorphins, serotonin, melatonin, and HGH (human growth hormone), and it lowers cortisol. And again, a little goes a long way. For the longest time, I believed I couldn't meditate—my mind was always too busy, I couldn't keep still, I felt like it wasn't doing anything or I wasn't doing it "right"—until I tried it for just five minutes a day. Anybody can sit still and breathe for five minutes, and I found that even that short practice made me calmer, less reactionary, and more at peace.

3. Epsom-salts and mineral-oil bath. Now, this is *definitely* self-care, but it does so much more than provide you with a quiet moment alone. Epsom salts contain sulfates, which trigger a process called reverse osmosis that pulls salt, toxins, and heavy metals out of your body. Epsom salts are also absorbed by your skin, replenishing your magnesium. Magnesium is incredible—it increases your serotonin levels and the ATP (energy) production of your cells, and it lessens the effects of adrenaline lingering in your body. Decorate your bathroom like a spa, play some music, light some candles, and simply luxuriate in detoxification bliss.

4. Social-media fast. This isn't easy for most of us, but it's so important. You know when you log on to Facebook just because you have a moment and you want to see what's going on, and then, before you know it, that "moment" has turned into 45 minutes? And they weren't even pleasurable? Social media has been found to sometimes create a sense of loneliness instead of the connection we seek. When all the connection we're receiving is reading about what other people are doing while we're sitting alone on our computer, then that clearly isn't real connection. So what do we do? All it takes is making a commitment to yourself not to log on. There's no need to uninstall the app from your phone—just don't look at it. Stay off of social media from 5 P.M. on, every day, or take 24 hours off once a week, or a week off once a month—and see how much better you feel.

5. Healing bodywork. I'm talking here about massage, acupuncture, Reiki, reflexology—whatever feels good. If it feels good to you, then that's the one to choose. And again this is about so much more than just a little self-love (though that is by no means a small thing). Traumatic events get stored up in your body—they can be big traumas, but they can also just be a fight you had with your sister that you can't seem to let go of. The reason you can't let go of it is that your body is holding on to it. Bodywork gets into the meridians, the *nadis,* the channels of energy in your body that can be blocked by these traumatic events, and clears them out so that they flow freely.

6. Breathing. Of course you breathe all day every day, but there are ways to breathe that do more than just provide you with the bare minimum of oxygen that you need. Think about it: increased oxygen equals increased energy. Spend just five minutes a day doing some breathing exercises that will slow your heart rate and lift your mood by raising your endorphin levels and lowering your stress hormones. Use your diaphragm to expand your belly, filling it as much as you can. Hold it for a count of five and release for a second count of five through your mouth. Practicing this kind of belly breathing for as little as five minutes a day oxygenates the cells of your body and your nervous system and increases your connection to Spirit—your prana.

7. Exercise. Take everything else in this list and put their effects on steroids, and you've got what exercise can do for you. Remember those stress chemicals we talked about earlier in this chapter? If you don't release them, they stay stuck in your body. Yes, exercise is absolutely important for maintaining bodily health, we all know that, but your brain needs it too. And it's so doable—there are several apps available that provide quick seven-minute workouts.

8. Laughter. The saying *laughter is the best medicine* is no joke—the act of laughing releases aggressive, negative energy trapped in the body, freeing up those feel-good chemicals like serotonin, as well as endogenous opioids that reduce pain in the body. Of course, there are times when we just don't feel like laughing. So help yourself out—go see a funny movie (it's impossible *not* to laugh at Melissa McCarthy), attend a stand-up comedy show, or even just sit and pretend to laugh for a few minutes—it really works! As laughter therapist Debra Joy Hart says, "If you are laughing, you are breathing. And that is a very good thing!"

9. Heart hugs. This is more than just a hug, and if you're a reluctant hugger like me, where I have to force myself to give a little two-second pat, it can be hard to do, but it's so powerful. Seek out a friend, someone you're comfortable with, and hug each other so that your hearts are aligned. Stay in this embrace for three whole breaths (it'll feel less awkward the more you do it). Like most true hugs, this will create a sense of connection and promote a sense of well-being. But it's also been proven to decrease anxiety, lower blood pressure, and stimulate oxytocin, serotonin, and dopamine.

10. Eight hours of sleep a night. Okay, we all want this one. The benefits of getting enough sleep are well-known. We get the *why*. It's the *how* that escapes us. Well, the good news is that everything else on this list will help you sleep better. Exercise, meditation, yoga—they've all been proven to improve your sleep. And cutting out social media in the evenings will get you away from that bright screen. There are other ways you can help yourself get the rest you need: take some melatonin, some valerian root, some L-tryptophan; I'm not suggesting taking Ambien or Halcion—L-tryptophan is the same stuff that's in a big turkey dinner. It's just enough to help your body get used to the idea of getting some good, restful sleep.

By sticking with doing one of these practices every day, one every week, and one every month, you will find that the results are exponential, forming a positive snowball effect of well-being.

In the next chapter, we're going to be talking about choices and probabilities. So far we've covered the three pillars of transforming our life—focus, beliefs, and chemistry—laying the groundwork so that we are ready to make different choices, changing our probabilities and potential outcomes.

CHAPTER 4

HOW TO MAKE CONSCIOUS CHOICES

"Change the way you look at things,
and the things you look at change."

— WAYNE DYER

In this chapter you will learn how to make decisions that will point you in the direction of your dreams and that will create the *you* you have always wanted to be. You will also learn how to break through your barrier beliefs and embrace change.

Now that you have an understanding of the way your physical body and the components of your brain work to control your life, it's important to emphasize that even though you might *think* circumstances or relationships in your reality are fixed, the truth is that anything is possible. Every day each choice you make unfolds even more possibilities and probable outcomes before you . . . if you're open to seeing something new.

SHAPING YOUR LIFE

As the lights dimmed in the recently restored Virginia The-atre in Champaign, Illinois, and the reel of the 1993 film *A Bronx Tale* started to play, I was immediately transported. Some friends and I were attending the renowned late film critic Roger Ebert's film festival—Ebertfest—an event that featured notably under-recognized films, each followed by a Q&A. According to Roger Ebert, *A Bronx Tale*, a gangster movie set in the '60s, was one such film.

Within the first 15 minutes of watching it, my friends and I recognized that it was a spiritual movie. The story follows a boy called "C," who was born and raised in the Bronx. C expe-rienced unconditional fatherly love both from his biological father, played by Robert De Niro, and from Sonny, the gangster who controlled the Bronx and who had taken C under his wing when he was only nine years old. The film's story spans almost a decade, and the lessons C learns from both his fathers seemed universal—each one more profound than the last.

The end of the film wraps the deep meaning of the story up in a few powerful lines said by C: "I learned to love and get love unconditionally; you just have to accept people for what they are. And I learned the greatest gift of all: the saddest thing in life is wasted talent, and the choices that you make will shape your life forever."

C's words were eerily impactful . . . and when the credits rolled, the audience's applause told me they felt it too. As the lights slowly came up, Chaz Ebert, Roger Ebert's widow, intro-duced the film's screenwriter, Chazz Palminteri, or "Chazz P" as Mrs. Ebert called him, for the Q&A session.

Out onto the stage before us walked the man who, five min-utes earlier, we'd seen as Sonny in the film's dramatic ending. The audience was stunned in disbelief.

"Hello, my name is C," he said.

For a few drawn-out seconds, silence rippled through the audience as he let us put things together by ourselves. The kid whose whole life had been so drastically changed by his choices, his father's guidance, and the influence of his gangster mentor, Sonny, stood there, proud, an authentic representation of the very words his character spoke just before the credits rolled. He was alive today because of those words. Those words had saved his life more times than he'd even known.

The choices that you make will shape your life forever.

I was intrigued at the depth of Chazz P's answers during the Q&A session. When it was over, my friends and I headed to the after-party at a local film production company. From the moment we walked in, I couldn't shake the thought that kept circling to the front of my mind. It felt like a broken record: *I hope Chazz P comes. I hope Chazz P comes. I hope Chazz P comes.*

When he walked in, I happened to have a direct line of sight of the front door. I saw everyone vying for his attention, but as I made my way toward the group surrounding him, he somehow noticed me.

I didn't want to waste his time with platitudes, so I said the first thing that came to mind when he looked at me and said hello: "I realize this is a gangster movie. But to me, this is a spiritual movie. This movie highlights how the choices we make in life control our probabilities."

That got his attention, and after he shook the hands of, thanked, and snapped photos with probably 25 people, he turned his attention back to me. I was standing aside from the group to wait, hoping I'd get a chance to talk more with him as the crowd thinned. Not a moment later, he gestured to me to follow him. I did, and before I knew it, Chazz Palminteri and I were in a side screening room at this production company, diving into a conversation about beliefs, probabilities, and choices, and how people don't realize just how powerful they are.

Well into our discussion, I told him about my dream of becoming an author. Chazz nodded softly to himself and then turned his head to me.

"It's not a coincidence we met. You're going to help people through writing books, I just know it." More than 20 years older now than he was in the film that put him on the map, he exuded the same kind of power and motivation that came through when he played Sonny the gangster, which made perfect sense, seeing how much he'd learned from the real Sonny the gangster.

I felt washed in pinch-me disbelief, gratitude, and validation. I thought back to the intense feelings I'd had during the movie, back to the emotion and shock I felt when Chazz stepped onstage and I realized it was based on the true events of his life, and then of the awe of the present moment of this conversation. I was seeing my own beliefs about the power of emotions and learning reflected back to me in real time.

In that conversation with Chazz, I saw that many powerful and successful people also acknowledged how important it was to be aware that each one of our choices can change our life forever. And it's the intensity of the emotion attached to each choice that shapes the strength of our will as well as our drive.

Life is *all* about choices, and if you can know that on an instinctual, powerfully emotional level, it makes it easier to start—and keep—paying attention to the choices you're making each and every day.

YOU CREATE YOUR LIFE

In earlier chapters we talked about how our moment-to-moment choices each day are all part of that 95 percent subconscious, autopilot programming. We also learned that this subconscious programming is the dominant force in our life—and if we want things in our life to be different, we have to make choices from our *conscious* mind, which only makes up an average of 5 percent of our daily thoughts.

Our choices make up our reality—they affect every single moment of every single day. Each time we make a conscious choice, we move forward in a new direction, one that opens us up to an infinite number of different outcomes. What determines our future are the micro-moments, the moment-to-moment choices that we make. And it's not even necessarily the biggest choices that have the most impact. Things like whether to go on a date, or whether to strike up a conversation; the decision to turn left or turn right when crossing the street—these choices can change your life. And it is these choices, informed by the emotional intensity behind them, that build our reality. We are our lives' architects, and every decision closes some doors and opens others.

EMBRACE THE CHANGE

Every time your heart beats, you are different. Every time you exhale, shift your weight from one foot to the other, or even smile, something changes within you. Every thought changes you as well, from moment to moment to moment, and you're not even aware of how much and how rapidly you're changing, even inside a 24-hour window.

If you were to observe a river, you'd see that it is constantly moving. But if you looked at it in snapshots taken a day, a week, month, or year apart, you won't see it changing. Yet over a period of time, a tree might get knocked down into the river, leaves will drop in from all over the region, and slowly, as the years roll by, the landscape of that river will become dramatically different. In fact, a single fallen tree in a river can completely change the direction of its flow, and this is without the river putting forth any effort at all. The river is just being a river.

We wouldn't notice the differences in the river from day to day, but we can understand that change is happening. We're experiencing a similar gradual change within ourselves. The biggest (and best) difference between us and the river, though, is that it doesn't take thousands of years for us to change our course. We are meant to experience accelerated personal evolution.

Like any other living, moving entity, human beings are not static creatures. We are changing with every blink of the eye, and though we're not consciously choosing how our heartbeats change us, or how our cells divide, or multiply, or die off, we *can* consciously make choices in other parts of our life. From what to have for lunch to how to invest our money, to when to run to the grocery store or where to go this weekend, every choice we make has an impact on our life.

Take a moment to notice two or three things that you are worrying about right now. For each one, trace your path back to the choices you made that led you to this moment. Sometimes you may need to go back decades. When I look at how I got to where I am now, I can trace it back to when I was 21 years old and was fired from my "dream job" at the bank because my personality was more "boss" than "employee." Especially since this was in the wake of grieving the death of my daughter, I was devastated. In fact, even though I began looking for another job right away, I became so depressed that I couldn't even imagine any other outcome or choice for my life than to take whatever job offer I got first, regardless of whether or not the job was a good fit for me. That job offer turned out to be for a telemarketing position.

When I think about that time and how it carved a path for me to reach today, I see how important that job choice was, though I didn't know it at the time. My experience as a telemarketer working within a scripted environment taught me how to create a scripted—and measurably effective—way to talk to people who owed me money when the economy tanked and people weren't able to pay their debts. From there, I created the program that I now call Conscious Communications, which I later started teaching to other companies as well as my own staff.

I wouldn't be here today if I had not taken that telemarketing job, as it changed the probable outcomes for everything else that would come into my life. I can trace where I am today back to that one moment, just as you may be able to do with the significant decisions you've made in your life.

CHOICES, BIG-D DECISIONS, AND LITTLE-D DECISIONS

You might be wondering: *How can I make the kinds of great choices that lead to me reaching outstanding probabilities?*

The answer to that question lies in your understanding of the power of decision. On a daily basis, if you're *deciding* or *choosing* what you're going to eat, there's no difference in those two words themselves. You can *choose* pasta for lunch or you can *decide* to have pasta for lunch; the idea is the same, whichever way you phrase it.

However, to Decide something (with a capital *D*, for emphasis) means you've charged the choice with intense emotion. Any Decision you make is connected to a pivot point that affects your future, and the power of that Decision comes from the intensity of the associated emotion.

The more you use your nervous system to make a Decision, the more power there will be behind your everyday choices. By contrast, when you are mostly making unconscious choices, the associated emotions aren't as intense; hence, there's not much power in them. If I make a Decision that's emotionally intense, with my desired outcome in mind, I have now mastered the connection between my desired outcome and my emotions.

For example, if I make a Decision to lose 20 pounds, a Decision that is connected to an intense emotion, this then becomes the springboard for me to make smaller choices that support the larger Decision. Bringing lunch to work instead of eating fast-food, and making sure to drink enough water, get enough sleep, and exercise can come from a place of motivation when they're inspired by the intensity of an emotion that's tied to a goal.

We all know that if someone says, "I should lose twenty pounds," there's no intensity behind that statement. By contrast, when a person says, "I've made the decision that I want to take my life and my health back; I'm going to lose twenty pounds," it's evident right away that this is a resolute Decision. This is an empowered statement, whereas the first is not.

While it's true that big Decisions create big changes in our life, the "little" ones are also impactful. These seemingly small decisions actually make a big difference in all areas of our life, but it's the most obvious in our relationships.

Say you've decided—subconsciously—you're too busy to put much energy into being mindful of your reactions toward your partner or your boss. That may mean you suffer in silence or that you're more irritable. No matter which you choose, both extremes of ignoring the impact of those small decisions about how to react can have massive and unfortunate ripple effects.

When you're in a situation where you have a bunch of unhealthy stress chemicals coursing through your body, that puts you in avidya. And once you're seeing things through the lens of misperception, you're much less likely to be able to evaluate those "small" decisions (like not reacting, choosing kindness, or being generous), and more likely to stay plugged in to the old programming that keeps you disconnected from a new set of possible outcomes. This is why we find it so powerful to reason things out with a friend—someone who you know will help you clear out the mental cobwebs—so you can find your peace again.

Here are a few other ideas to try when you feel you "don't have any other choice" but to react negatively to an unwanted situation:

- **Meditate.** Find a quiet place and spend some time with your thoughts.

- **Take a bath or a shower (even if you're already clean).** Take advantage of the relaxing power of water.

- **Cut back on the caffeine intake.** Caffeine is a stimulant and can cause nervousness, irritation, and high blood pressure.

- **Go to the gym.** Work off some of that crankiness.

- **List your choices.** Make a list of what you think your choices are, and reach out to someone who can weigh in and help you find an alternate perspective.

- **Fake it till you make it.** Practice saying something joyful (even if it's unrelated to your situation) instead of swirling in sarcastic or inflammatory thoughts and statements. This will plant a seed of hope in you instead of cultivating the feelings of dread.

- **Apply the 10-10-10 rule.** Ask yourself, *How is this situation going to affect me in the next ten days, ten weeks, or ten years?* This helps you measure the impact of both the situation and the way you're reacting to it.

- **Check yourself.** Ask yourself if your chosen reaction in that moment is lined up with your long-term goals. If the answer is no, you have an opportunity to explore what choice or decision *would* be in line with your long-term goals and then to move in that direction.

FOCUS ON THE NOW

If there's ever a time when you're at a crossroads and you're not sure what choice to make, try to step aside and ask yourself these questions:

- *What do I* really *want to happen here?*

- *What do I want right now, and what do I want in the long run?*

- *Are the two matched up (in alignment)?*

These questions will help you discern what to do in the present, even if you're unclear about your ultimate or long-term desires. Often the most honest answer you can find is *I want to be happy,* because when it comes down to it, almost everything we want is because we believe it's going to make us feel better. Using *I want to be happy* as the baseline makes it easier to filter your choices. Let's take, for example, a woman who is deciding between two jobs. The one position comes with a great salary and high prestige, but a stressful environment—she knows it will be a struggle to get out of bed every morning. The other job has a lower salary but the work is inspiring and the atmosphere supportive. There's no "right" decision but, in making a choice, it's important for her to ask herself where she'll be most happy. When we're happy, we thrive, and that affects everything around us, including the moment-by-moment choices we make, creating unanticipated opportunities now and in the future.

Choosing a job is an important crossroads in life, but the same principle can be applied to smaller choices as well. The other day I decided to meet a friend for coffee, something I knew would make me happy. Not only did we have a great time, but it soon became a lively brainstorming session; it was so productive, in fact, that we both left with multiple ideas on how to make our respective businesses even more successful. This small, (seemingly) insignificant choice unintentionally moved me closer to realizing my long-term goals.

Starting with happiness as your goal, I want you to take a minute to fill in the six bullet points below. Honestly ask yourself, *What things would need to be true in my life in order for me to be happy right now?*

We'll start out with a few common responses to get you going:

- Spending quality time with friends and family.
- Taking a vacation.
- Achieving a personal goal.
-
-
-
-
-
-

The six things you wrote down are the areas you need to focus on in order to move forward. The idea is that the essence of what we want is happiness, and everything else we desire is in support of that. Let's say one of your bullet items was "more loving relationships," for example. You can use that simple goal to pause and filter your responses and choices so you can experience more connection with those around you, even as you work to rewrite old programming. Using your desire as the filter for how you make choices is a way to set your course, your intention, just like a sailor would set his coordinates to make sure he is steering his ship in the right direction.

Setting your intention—that is, to make a Decision that's powered by intense emotions and focus—is one of the most important aspects of this work you're doing. There are many things you can do to set your intention, but only you know the ways to plug your desires into the intense emotional charge that will affect your thinking, your words, your actions, your life, and the lives of those around you.

Setting an intention that carries an intense emotional charge, plus making a Decision, supercharges your manifesting powers. Focus on your present moment, your *now*, and you'll be able to quickly sort through the choices that do and don't work for you. This is the start of living a more authentically driven life.

HOW YOUR CHOICES AFFECT YOUR PROBABILITIES

It might seem obvious by now that each choice you make, whether on a small or large scale, can and does affect your life. There's beauty in this, because it means we have the freedom to create our reality with every action that we take. We have the free will to make choices, and if we are making choices based on whether they'll connect or disconnect us to our core desires, our life will feel better as we move up the frequency scale.

That's not to say you should shirk your responsibilities or necessary tasks as you focus on your core desires. *Psychology Today* reported that the physical checking off of goals on a to-do list will release dopamine, one of the most pleasurable of the happy hormones in our body. They state that one main reason to break down tasks into achievable goals is in order to identify their beginning, middle, and end. Even if you're not that jazzed about the chore itself, your body will reward you for completing it. But you also must be willing to say no when you mean it. For example, agreeing to a lunch invitation from that "friend" you don't like all that much will only move you down the frequency scale and away from creating the life you're working so hard to remake.

Every thought you think, every word you speak, and every choice you make is creating your world and the way you perceive it. Making a "little" decision to send your gratitude messages to your group, checking off one of the stress busters in your Zen 10, working on your 100 Things list, or even going to the grocery store—they all make a difference in the end. You can create your world however you imagine it to be.

We often put our needs toward the bottom of our priority list each day, when we need to be putting them at the top—to make choices 100 percent according to what we want, instead of what others want for us or what we think we *should* want for ourselves.

Once when I came to this point at a workshop, a woman in the second row raised her hand up high, waving it all around to stop me.

She said, "It sounds to me like you're telling us to be selfish."

I answered, "If you want to move the needle of change in your life, you've *got* to be a little selfish . . . there's no way around it."

Naturally she looked confused, but I'll tell you what I told her and the rest of the audience that day: There is a big difference between being selfish and practicing healthy self-care, which goes beyond the occasional manicure. If you were to ask yourself the question, *What do I want?* and if you lived 100 percent of your time according to what you really wanted, you'd be operating from an empowered sense of self, and you'd be happier, more excited about life, and more eager to grow and learn and try new things. Imagine how doing this would totally shift the probable results or outcomes in your life. Living your life this way, making decisions 100 percent of the time based on what you really desire, is a powerful concept. It requires you to choose yourself, at all times. If you can train yourself to meet your own needs and desires first, those around you—including the world at large—won't be able to escape the light you'll radiate.

Take steps to be in control of your choices rather than letting them control you. This can only be done when you're able to identify what it is you want in the present moment—your *now* moment, as meditation teachers sometimes say. If you're not focused on the present moment (if you're resenting the past or worrying about the future), it's guaranteed that you'll feel unhappy with the outcome of the probabilities before you. The true place of power comes from being present with yourself and your thoughts and feelings—your now moment. All that matters is what you're choosing right now.

Understanding this is important, and it's often glossed over in a person's race to improve him- or herself. The best thing you can do for yourself is to make choices that are in alignment with your desires, as this is what molds your probabilities to line up with your inner world. This doesn't mean you should be a self-absorbed jerk; in fact, often our desires and what makes us happy center on helping others.

Whatever is happening right now is connecting us to a future that matches this now moment. Every slice of now connects us to a certain probability or future. And though this is impossible to measure, some wisdom teachers suggest we switch probable realities thousands of times each minute, shifting probabilities even because of each thought we think.

The emotions and energy that linger in your mind and body, even when you're not actively making a choice, can guide and determine probable outcomes. Being present means connecting to your feelings, to your thoughts, and to your body's sensations. For example, are you enjoying your chocolate cake, being in the moment, or are you thinking about the calories, even feeling shame or guilt from eating it?

What you focus on grows. So it comes down to training your focus, which is a skill we have been working with since Chapter 1. When you are living in the moment, what you're seeing, feeling, or experiencing will more powerfully connect you to a set of exciting, desirable outcomes.

BREAK THROUGH BARRIER BELIEFS

"For every action, there is an equal and opposite reaction."

— NEWTON'S THIRD LAW OF MOTION

Newton's third law of motion applies to more than just physical objects. If we extend the principle out to explain other laws of motion—like, *what goes up must come down*—we can start to see that, for every choice we make, there is an associated outcome or result. It's not a mystical or magical or ethereal concept; it's physics.

Now, I'm not suggesting you overhaul every area of your life at once—nor am I suggesting you avoid this. *You're* steering this ship! What I am asking is that you take just one step in the direction of your desire . . . and see how even a small pivot can not only change the way you feel about something, but it can also completely shift your probable outcomes.

So what does it mean to take "a step in the direction" of your desire? What might that look like? To begin with I'll emphasize that this step is the cliché "baby step" of making new choices. Make that phone call you've put off, open up to a conversation you need to have, or complete that task that's been hanging around on your to-do list. It doesn't have to be earth-shattering. When you take even a small step in the direction of your desire, you'll be surprised how much new zest for life it will infuse into your day.

One of the things I've noticed is that people get all kinds of ideas, but they rarely take action on any of them. Instead, they *talk* about what they *should* do, what they're *trying* to do . . . but they never *do*. As C said in *A Bronx Tale*, "The saddest thing in life is wasted talent, and the choices that you make will shape your life forever."

What if taking a step in the direction of your desire meant doing some research on that patent idea you had? Or sitting closer to that hot guy you met at a friend's birthday party? When you make the Decision to lose 20 pounds, you've charged that desire with intense emotion. Generally the intensity fades over time, and taking action in that direction might get more and more difficult if you're not making renewed daily commitments to keep your focus aligned with your desired outcome. Not wanting to go to the gym but going anyway, or not wanting to order the salad dressing on the side but doing it anyway, can be steps in the right direction. The steps you take need to be in alignment with the outcome that you want, and this is what gets you closer to that probability becoming the most likely one. By changing your lifestyle, you've changed your probable outcomes too. These aren't *massive* choices, but movement on them is one of the most important ingredients for creating a new probable outcome in your life.

If it's that simple, why don't we do it?

There's a simple answer: our barrier beliefs. A barrier or brick-wall belief will stop us dead in our tracks, keeping us from taking action.

Massive action starts with breaking through!

What does it mean to take massive action? It means to take the drastic and deliberate steps necessary to propel us out of our comfort zones, a conscious decision to take action that will bring us closer to our dreams and life goals. It means following our intuition and taking a leap of faith because our desire is more powerful than our fear. Massive action is the actual steps involved, and, for each one of us, the challenge will be different. It could be initiating a conversation with someone we're terrified to approach or booking a ticket to go someplace we've never been. It could be the decision to submit a manuscript for publication, or the choice to quit law school in order to pursue a degree in baking. It means we stop worrying about being 100 percent perfect, and, instead, summon the courage to break through those barrier beliefs and move toward our dreams.

Our actions (whether we take just a step or do something massive) will either connect us or disconnect us with the life we want. Like Legos that build upon one another, our daily 60,000 thoughts, whether good or bad, are what we build and create our life with. Our choices and probabilities line up to redirect our life, but this only happens when we're taking action.

WHAT'S THE RIGHT CHOICE?

How do you know when one choice is better than another?

The correct choice has resonance—but not in the standard definition of the word. To me resonance means to have a knowing about something, a knowing so deep that you feel it in every cell in your body. It means connecting with your frequency scale, your intuition. You know the feeling I'm talking about? Trust it.

Here are a few more specific ways to know when one choice is better for you than another:

1. Between the available choices, one will more clearly connect you to your ultimate goal.

2. One choice just feels good, better, or more exciting.

3. One choice will create enthusiasm, which opens you up to feeling the building momentum. And because of that feeling, you know this choice will inspire you to want to reach for even more.

4. Sometimes all available options seem painful, even the choice not to make a choice. Examples of this would be deciding when to put down a pet who is suffering, or when to leave a relationship with someone you love but who isn't right for you anymore. In these cases the better choice is the one that, though difficult and painful, will offer relief.

And sometimes we just haven't thought of all the possibilities. Sometimes we're too caught up in a situation to see that there might be a *different,* better choice available. Try taking a step back. The point is that you get to choose, and you get to choose it all.

BRINGING IT ALL TOGETHER

Everything you experience in your life is controlled by your thoughts. The choices that present themselves to you are created by your thoughts. Not the other way around. Whatever thoughts you're thinking today will show up for you in your reality, and when this happens you have a choice to make.

I want you to understand how powerful your emotions are. When you can link up to the charge of the emotion of happiness, for example, you can effect more change both for yourself and for those around you than if you're just *blah* about a choice you've got to make. An intensely happy feeling has a powerful effect on the way you see the world as well as the choices you'll make because of it.

In the same way that the intensity of positive emotions can have a dramatic impact on the probable outcomes of our life, so too can the intensity of negative emotions. Too often, we feel uncomfortable emotions and want them to go away. We need to learn to sit with and experience our emotions, whatever they may be. What's more, the darker, more shadowy emotions can tell us things about ourselves if we're willing to listen. Sweeping our emotional darkness under a positivity-colored rug is a terrible idea. In fact, doing this is like trying to hold an enormous beach ball underwater in the pool. We can get it to stay down (sort of) for a bit, but it won't be long before we lose our grip and it launches back up above the water, shocking us and everyone else who's watching. When we're not feeling positive, we need to listen to that feeling. There are powerful lessons woven into our emotions—whether they're intensely positive *or* negative . . . or anywhere else on the spectrum. We just have to pay attention.

If you make your choices based on how you feel, you will make better decisions, and these decisions will lead you down roads of synchronicity. Following your emotions is like using your own inner GPS. Remember from Chapter 3 that your emotions are created because of a message your nervous system receives, so if you feel bad about something, there's a reason. It's scary to listen to our feelings in these situations, but being present with them helps us create more aligned choices.

When, in this process of feeling your way through your choices, you recognize you've set an arbitrary boundary or are limiting yourself by your own barrier belief, you've gotten a glimpse into a probability you couldn't see before. Celebrate that win. Find a thread of gratitude for your ability to choose to see another choice, and watch as each day you feel better and better.

EXERCISE: THE BIG 10

Open to a new page in your journal and write down a bullet-point list of 10 major things you remember from your life that had a big impact on you.

Then pick one of the bullets points and set a timer for 10 minutes.

Start with *I remember . . .* and tell the story of the memory you chose. Tell it in a way that connects it to where you are today.

Here's my example of this exercise, so you have a reference for it:

I remember getting fired from the bank. I remember how afraid I was to tell my boyfriend. I remember I felt like a big loser. I'd always believed I would amount to nothing and now it was official. What would my life be today if I hadn't been fired? Honestly, I don't think any detail would have been the same. Would I have met my husband? No, probably not. Would I have moved away? It's a burning desire for me to understand life and how this all works.

When I was a young girl, I had big dreams. I understand now that I couldn't have lived my big dreams if I hadn't got 10 fired. Losing that job opened the door to a new one. I couldn't have known it at the time, but the skills I learned telemarketing were what I later used to build my thriving business, which eventually led to a desire to make a change in the industry.

Every step we take, every choice we make ultimately shapes our future. I can connect all the dots and trace my life back to that moment sitting in the bank getting canned.

You can unpack more than just one of the memories on your list (and you might want to, if this inspires you). As you can see, the results of this exercise should be a more personalized understanding of how interconnected the events, conversations, chance meetings, opportunities, and seasons in our life really are. It is true that we co-create our own reality, and if we want our reality to be different, we must *do* something different. But it doesn't take much to move the needle of change in our life.

When you step out of the established default choices that you *should* or *could* take, you'll create a new neural pathway that'll reroute you in a different direction—one that will (inevitably) present you with new opportunities and possibilities and feed your bonfire of desire.

In the next chapter, we'll learn about how important our choices are when it comes to the day-to-day maneuverability of our lives, and how the simple act of choosing can take us closer to, or farther from, our own personal mountain.

CHAPTER 5

TO CLEANSE OR TO CLOG, THAT IS THE QUESTION

*"We are products of our past,
but we don't have to be prisoners of it."*

— RICK WARREN

In the previous chapter, you saw my moving conversation with writer and actor Chazz Palminteri and his charge to me about choices and how our choices affect the probable outcomes of our life. Throughout my exchange with Chazz, he emphasized that despite the different experiences each of us has, our responses to those experiences—and our choices going forward—are what shape our life. These are the moments that define what is probable and possible for our futures. This chapter will help you define which habits in your life are beneficial for creating your ideal life and learn how to change the habits that are bringing you down.

BECOMING A SPIRITUAL WARRIOR

At the after-party for *A Bronx Tale,* Chazz and I had been talking for about an hour when his team peeked their heads in to check on him and usher him back to his hotel. It was getting late, and despite it being a weekend, both of us needed to wrap up the evening.

Before getting up, he paused and gently shook his head. "Mary, this moment was supposed to happen. You're a spiritual warrior. And if you're going to stay true to that, you've got to keep your vessel clean."

Instantly, I knew exactly what he meant and that it didn't have as much to do with diet and exercise as much as it had to do with my mental state. But the part about me being a spiritual warrior struck me with an unfamiliar pull. I wanted to be a spiritual warrior, though at times I saw myself more as a mixed martial arts warrior, someone who was more comfortable in spandex and a kickboxing class, than the spiritual kind.

"Thank you, Chazz," I said. "I want you to know how much it means to me that we've been able to talk like this, and how grateful I am to have spent this time with you." I smiled, somehow hoping it would match the validation I felt inside. Instead of going on about his accomplishments, successes, world-changing ideas, or any other agenda he might've had, Chazz had sat with me at *his* movie's after-party and was more interested in talking to me about my vision for helping others with my book than anything else. I was moved at his selflessness.

As he stood to leave, he approached me with open arms and wrapped me in a hug, just as warm as if we'd known one another our whole lives and might even see each other for a family dinner the next week.

When he pulled himself back, he looked me squarely in the face: "Don't forget this conversation. Don't forget what I told you."

I smiled and nodded, a chill coming over me. It reminded me of the feeling Chazz must've had as the kid whose life his film was based on. A chill to the bone, with the knowledge that you're receiving orders from someone more powerful than you—maybe like the gangster he played in the movie—who was invested, who cared.

He added, "I need you to know how special you are. It was no coincidence that we met." He smiled kindly, his face not betraying any 1 A.M. after-party exhaustion, and with that he left.

Not more than a month earlier, I had sat at my first Hay House Writer's Workshop, which was where I committed to writing this book and sharing these tools with more people. Even though after our conversation I didn't immediately see the ripple effect of Chazz's words, they felt like confirmation that I was on the right path.

I got home around 2 o'clock in the morning, still pretty wired from the whole evening. I lay in bed, staring up at the ceiling, and couldn't help but replay our conversation, feeling the excitement of how it affirmed everything from my passion for helping others grow to the hope of growing my own business in unique ways. It didn't seem to matter how many sheep I tried counting; nothing relaxed me enough to be able to sleep. And then, suddenly, my mind raced backward into a memory that made everything click.

LIVING LIFE BY THE 80/20 RULE

Every time I reach for a bite of food, I ask myself, *Will this cleanse me or clog me?* If the answer is *clog*, I make a more conscious choice about indulging. It doesn't mean I won't indulge, but rather that I would let go of wanting my diet, and myself, to be perfect. The very idea of perfection is a clog in itself because it lacks balance. Anything imbalanced—even on the positive side—is an indication you are living in extremes.

Without much prompting, I soon found myself linking cleanse-or-clog alongside the "80/20 principle", which naturally fit together. My personal explanation and use of the 80/20 rule would be desserts (or even a *bite* of a dessert) going into the "20 percent of my intake" column, and healthy choices going in the "80 percent column." Even still, I also knew there were other areas in life where people could apply the filter of cleanse or clog:

behaviors and choices that were either connecting them to or disconnecting them from the future that they want and about which they dream. For example, if you're wasting a lot of energy in a toxic relationship with a friend, a boyfriend, or a girlfriend, and you know it's draining you, it's a disconnect or a clog.

We'll go into this in more detail as we move along, but I want to give you three questions you can ask yourself when you need clarity about which things are clogging and disconnecting you from your desired future.

Consider an aspect of your life that could be a cleansing activity, relationship, or habit, or a clogging one. Once you have it in your mind, I want you to hit RESET on your preconceived ideas about this soon-to-be-evaluated behavior or choice. Start by surveying its aftermath, the results you're getting from the experience, and then look at the outcome. Is your behavior or choice causing more harm than good? For example, imagine you're a salsa dancer, and nowhere else do you feel that magical zest for life but when you're on the dance floor. The only problem is, the best dance studio with a salsa night is three towns over, and in order to make it work, you have to organize your household (kids, partner, pets, and perhaps even work) to get by in your absence. Sometimes it feels easier to skip salsa dancing to avoid the headache that comes with the planning. But is it *really* easier?

A fast and easy measurement of a cleanse or a clog is to acknowledge whether you feel better or worse after going dancing (in our example), and whether you feel the aftermath of your night out is either worth every minute of it, or that it drains you of your energy.

If you aren't sure, ask yourself:

1. *Does going dancing (doing this habit of mine/thinking this way/choosing this response) connect me to or disconnect me from what I want, from my goals, or from my values?* (Hint: You can apply this question to everything!)

2. *On a scale of 1–10, how important is it for me to engage in this behavior or make this choice?* Wherever it ranks on the 1–10 scale, ask yourself why. Why does it rank so high or low? Maybe your reasons are legitimate. But if you answer with a 2 and you still go ahead and do it anyway, you're going against your internal compass. This is another way to get off track, disconnect from your desired future, and clog your energy from opening up possible outcomes.

3. *Is it really what I need?* Maybe you ranked your choice or habit high on the 1–10 scale, but you know that despite its importance, it's still unnecessary. If you don't really *need* to go dancing—or whatever the individual activity, choice, or habit in question is— earmark it for now and we'll come back to it.

Only you—the most honest-with-yourself version of you— can answer these questions. As we go along, you'll have even more clarity on the areas in your life that aren't serving you, how you can change them, and how you can prioritize the things in your life that help cleanse.

GOING BACK TO THE FREQUENCY SCALE

The most important indicator of cleanse or clog is the way you feel about something, plain and simple. Recently I heard that one of my employees needed a car but didn't feel worthy of a regular car loan. Mind you, she hadn't even checked her credit score. Because of this limiting belief, she took a limited action and bought a car from what we call a "buy here, pay here" dealership. The car isn't great, her interest rate is astronomically high, and making that choice only reaffirmed her self-doubt—which, ironically, wasn't based on facts.

Not long after she and I began working on this belief, her life slowly pivoted. When she had to move into a new apartment, she was able to sign a lease on the apartment of her dreams, only to have the leasing agent say: "Well, I *know* we don't have to worry about you skipping out! You are our collection agent!" This employee had always been reliable, and this moment reflected that truth back to her—but only because she was feeling better and could actually see the truth. Regardless of what *is* or *was,* how she felt was what determined her outcome—and that's where it always starts.

The same can be said for wellness. If you are overweight, consider how you feel about thin people. If you refer to them as "skinny bitches," for example, that is a major clog. But if you can refer to thin, healthy, or fit people without judging them (which is basically judging yourself), you're inching closer to being able to feel better about your weight and yourself, moving up the frequency scale.

As we went over in Chapter 3, the frequency scale is a measurement of your emotions. When you're trending upward on it, you're feeling better, and trending down means you're feeling worse. Based on your frequency, you'll attract experiences that match your emotions, so it's always best to keep your eye on that frequency scale.

Do you have 20 pounds to lose? Don't shame yourself over it. "Perfection" is not the only picture of health. Instead, find a way to dwell on what's great about your body so you can move up on that frequency scale, feel better, and attract better-feeling circumstances and experiences. The point of this is that if we can look in the mirror and love our body as it is, we will experience a cleanse. And looking at our body in any other way, in any less-than-loving way, creates a clog. The way you feel about it—your body, your health, your life, your bank account, your *whatever it is*—determines whether you're undergoing a cleanse or a clog.

Often people move farther up the frequency scale when they make cleansed, connected choices, which encourages them to feel even better. Or they make clogging and disconnecting choices, which moves them down the scale into feeling even worse. Seeing this led me to ask two questions:

1. *Why do we so often gravitate toward clogging foods, friendships, or situations?*

2. *Why do we not automatically choose the ones that make us feel better, that cleanse us, and that connect us to the futures we so sincerely desire?*

After looking deeply at these questions and thinking about the brain, I saw that the answer was simple: we default to these choices because of our programming. Most of us were brought up with (and have become accustomed to) making unconscious, disconnected lifestyle choices—and if we knew better, we'd do better. The problem is, *we just don't know better.*

The pattern of choosing a clog, or disconnection, reaffirms the neural pathway dedicated to that choice, and the more often we choose a clog, the easier it becomes to choose that clog again and again. So even if we sense our choice is moving us down that frequency scale toward feeling worse, and away from our desired outcomes, if we don't consciously interrupt the pattern, we default to our programming. To interrupt it we must awaken to the fact that our life is forever tethered to how our desires—and subsequent choices—move us up or down the frequency scale.

In order to move closer to those desires, we have to feel good enough to even consider what our desires might be. But in order to feel good, we have to keep our mind and body connected. Two things remain true about keeping your vessel clean: First, there are a number of activities that are neutral in and of themselves. They can either cleanse *or* clog you, and your mind-set when you use or engage with them is what determines whether they are a cleanse or a clog. Second, beyond those 50/50 neutral activities, you need to get clear on what the big cleansers and cloggers are in the major areas of life.

To begin unpacking those, here are a few common 50/50 activities that can be either cleansers or cloggers:

Television. Are you sitting in front of the TV for extended periods of time, thoughtlessly drifting into an alpha brain-wave state but not enjoying the alpha benefits? This is a clog. On the flip side, coming home after a long day and taking your shoes off in front of the TV while you decompress for 15 or 20 minutes can be a cleanse.

Attending a social event. If you want to go to the event in question, it can be fun. If you're in this space, attending will mean connecting with your desires and with other people, and it will open you up to invite in even more new experiences. This is a cleanse. By contrast, if you don't want to attend the event—or even if you do want to but you're pressed for time and using your evening that way would be an added stressor—attending will be a clog. It will disconnect you from yourself and from other possible outcomes that would have been more in line with your desire.

Drinking coffee or wine. Studies have shown health benefits to consuming both of these beverages regularly. Having a cup of coffee in the morning and a glass of red wine in the evening—even as often as every day—can be a cleanse. But having four to six cups of coffee in the morning, more throughout the day, and a bottle of wine at night before bed? Definitely a clog.

As you can see, if it's extreme, no matter what it is, it's not a cleanse, and it won't connect you to any of the ultimate feelings you're striving for. Granted, there are many more of these 50/50 activities, and you likely have a few that are not listed above. It doesn't matter what you're doing in one of these either/or activities, as long as you're focused on making it a cleanse rather than a clog.

Next I'll show you a breakdown of the six biggest areas in life: health, finances, career, personal relationships, self-care, and spirituality. Within them, I've listed activities or habits that can be considered cleansing choices or clogging ones. Of course, I can't think of every way you are cleansing or clogging in your life, so if you don't see one of your cleanses or clogs here, celebrate your uniqueness! I want to encourage you to read through the activities and see what resonates with you—no matter if it's a cleanse or a clog—as this will prepare you for the exercise at the end of the chapter that aims to help you find your balance.

BE AWARE OF YOUR HEALTH

"The first wealth is health."

— RALPH WALDO EMERSON

We've talked about health at length already in this chapter and the preceding chapters, so to keep you running at full steam here, I'll keep this category simple and brief. Take a look at the following two lists and see which of your daily habits around your whole-body wellness fall under cleanse and which ones fall under clog.

CLEANSE	CLOG
Getting plenty of sleep (aim for at least eight hours!)	Staying up late zoning out in front of the TV or computer
Exercising (morning stretches, yoga, running, etc.)	Frequently consuming over-the-counter pills to alleviate ills triggered by food, such as antacids and proton pump inhibitors
Drinking lots of water (until you pee like a racehorse!)	Eating large amounts of fried, frosted, frozen, boxed, or fake food (double-dog clog—it affects your finances *and* your health!)
Eating apples, bananas, avocados, spinach, kale, and other dark green leafy veggies	Abusing alcohol and smoking cigars or cigarettes (double-dog clog—you're spending money while harming your health!)

Loading up on protein (it's a key to building muscle), and eating yogurt (great source of probiotics)	Bingeing on sugary energy bars or sugary coffee drinks
Using medicinal herbs, like cilantro or oregano, or taking omegas	Drinking soda (even diet soda!)
Experiencing a mind-blowing orgasm (great way to reset your nervous system)	Eating foods labeled "low fat" or "diet"

At your first glance over these two lists, it should be clear that the clogging choices are linked to poor overall health. You can make a change in a heartbeat—so don't be intimidated. This is going to be easier than you think, as every single itty-bitty change is going to make your life better and will change your probabilities.

Changing ourselves on a core level goes back to our neural pathways, to our internal brain patterning . . . also known as our programming or wiring. But knowing what we want to rewrite is the only way we can even begin to change our programming. Awareness is the key to the doors of freedom.

FEEL GOOD ABOUT YOUR FINANCES

"Recast your current problems into proactive goals."

— SUZE ORMAN

Financial clogs can be huge triggers for us, as they're often coping mechanisms for other deep-seated fears we have about safety and security. Nevertheless, the biggest financial clog I see time and time again is how people *feel* about their finances.

Following are some cleanses and clogs, and I would invite you to let your eyes linger on the items that stand out in this list. Even if you don't think you're clogged in one area, if your eyes catch on something, take note. And remember that the brain is often smarter than we give it credit for.

CLEANSE	CLOG
Creating a budget and starting a nest egg for your future	Ignoring that retirement is coming (when it is)
Checking your credit report three times a year (*see page 114)	Acting like you won the lottery with your tax refund, or paying extra to get it now (double-dog finance clog—you wasted money to get the payment early and didn't use the refund wisely)
Paying off your credit cards *every* month, and paying your taxes on time	Shopping when emotional or triggered ("retail therapy")
Asking the right questions and doing your research before refinancing your home or making a big financial decision	Spending more than you earn
Treating yourself to a new outfit for an upcoming event (double-bonus cleanse—it will increase your confidence, which will give you a boost, and possibly help you make a connection at the event!)	Holding on to your storage unit (are the contents worth the cost of the unit?)
Checking out rummage and estate sales, and finding amazing buys at second-hand stores	Maxing out your credit cards during the holidays
Shopping for groceries on a full stomach	Shopping for groceries when hungry
Going out to a fabulous, mind-stimulating dinner with friends (double-bonus cleanse: for your health *and* your relationships)	Eating out for convenience

*I'm passionate about credit reporting—it's my field, after all—and so I wanted to include this special pro-tip. You'll want to visit www.annualcreditreport.com to request a free credit report. Note: There are three credit bureaus—Equifax, TransUnion, and Experian—and you can get one copy of each bureau's report per year. I suggest picking a time each year when you'll request your report from each—for example, New Year's Day, your birthday, and Labor Day. The really great news is that if you find an inaccuracy, you can dispute it right then and there, and what you dispute on one is automatically disputed on all three. This makes finding and disputing inaccuracies uber-efficient. The best part is, the U.S. government mandates that these bureaus provide credit reports for the public—and that the service must be free. If you take advantage of it, you'll never again have to pay for a copy of your credit report.

For people without proper financial training or experience, simply broaching this subject can ignite the fight-or-flight adrenaline response. But this area of life is where the treasure is—and how you feel, think, speak, and act on your choices determines the direction you're guiding your ship. In the interest of cleansing the areas in your life that have more clog than you'd like, it is necessary to shine a light there. Doing so will make it easier for you to move up that frequency scale, feel better, and reprogram brain patterns away from fear-based financial thinking and planning and toward abundance, prosperity, and financial freedom.

YOU ARE MORE THAN YOUR CORNER OFFICE

"Success is nothing more than a few simple disciplines, practiced every day; while failure is simply a few errors in judgment, repeated every day."

— JIM ROHN

Whether we're content to be employees, destined to be CEOs or entrepreneurs, or somewhere in between, most of us have to work. That being said, are you unhappy at work? Are you getting passed up for promotions? Do you feel discontent, unfulfilled, or stuck? If your answer is yes to any of these, you might ask your-self how you did on the last project your boss gave you—was it your best work? And are you at work on time every day? How's your attendance? Your general attitude?

I'd like to encourage you to look at the following cleanse or clog ideas and, if you feel unhappy or discontent in any way in your career, see what resonates with you. We'll circle back to this later, so make sure to flag the topics that stand out to you the most.

CLEANSE	CLOG
Being solution oriented and thinking outside the box	Complaining
Utilizing (or creating!) standardized communications for consistency	Needing constant monitoring
Exceeding expectations (major cleanse—people will know they can count on you, which will further your career, and lead to new opportunities!)	Having a consistently negative attitude
Dressing to impress—look the part you want to play	Looking sloppy
Making your job your mission	Wasting time at the proverbial water cooler
Collaborating with co-workers as a team player	Gossiping
Contributing and giving back to the culture and community of your workplace	Being late to work or calling in sick when you're not sick

Making your co-workers look good (major cleanse—when you do things for other people, they may reciprocate, helping you look good and furthering your own career!)	Missing or forgetting deadlines
Creating genuine connections with customers and co-workers	Making excuses, not taking responsibility, or saying, "That's not my job"
Owning up to your mistakes or screw-ups	Being a difficult person to work with
Being easy to work with	Being confrontational or inflexible
Understanding and doing what's expected of you	Stealing time and money by using personal social media accounts while at work (major clog—you're not as productive, it makes you look bad, and it could even get you fired!)

As the boss I have to wear lots of hats, but my eyes are never far from identifying which of my employees are more clogged than cleansed. From my perspective it makes my job and my life more enjoyable when I'm working with proactive, driven, happy, and cleansed individuals. And I know that if I'm happy to work with the people on my team, my team is more likely to be happy to work with one another.

One thing I like to do at work is run wacky, fun, and exciting incentive programs to help my staff connect with each other and to keep our office morale high—which is something I wish more companies (especially collection companies) did more of. Recently we had a monthlong, companywide contest to see who wrote the most thank-you cards. That person would be rewarded with a gift card to a local smoothie bar.

When the month was over, the corkboard in the break room was overflowing with these thank-you cards, and the number of cards written and received was remarkable. You know just how wonderful it feels to give (and get) a thank-you card, and that feeling of generosity in giving and receiving filled our office with more than just words scribbled on hand-cut cards made from unused cardstock. The contest infused the office with gratitude, it made work more fun for my staff, and it created better relationships between the employees, which helped change their mind-set about work for a number of them. At the end of the month, it wasn't even a little bit about who got the gift card. It was about cultivating the culture of connecting . . . which was a major, *major* cleanse.

BITE YOUR EVIL TONGUE

"Everything in our lives is predicated on the quality of our relationships."

— TONY ROBBINS

Regardless of who we think we are and the saints we may have in our life, there is often at least one relationship where we find ourselves triggered in our conversations or interactions. We say the nastiest things (and "nasty" is relative to your personal standards), we react in ways we're not proud of, and because we slipped into behavior we don't like, we almost always feel guilty afterward. In those moments of reflection when we feel that guilt, we might also find ourselves asking the following questions:

- *Did I really need to be the one who was right?*
- *Couldn't I have just let that go?*
- *Could I have responded more appropriately or with more kindness?*

I want to assure you that interactions in our personal relationships are more likely to get the leftover silt in our emotional tank at the end of the day than any of our other interactions. Notably, it's in our personal relationships that we feel the safest and mouth off the quickest, but this isn't an excuse to rationalize a clog.

One of the more insidious ways to destroy trust and relationships—whether it is with a lover, a friend, or a family member—is through engaging in something called *lashon hara*. This is a Hebrew term that literally translates into "evil tongue." The phrase *lashon hara* means "to gossip," but more specifically, it means to lead someone to gossip through manipulation. For example, let's say Abby runs into Dana, a friend who she knows has a bad relationship with another woman in the neighborhood, Jennifer. As soon as Abby sees Dana, she makes a point of telling her that she saw Jennifer in the coffee shop the other day. Technically, Abby isn't gossiping—however, she *is* purposefully bringing up the topic of conversation with the specific intent to get Dana to gossip. If you find yourself in even the subtlest versions of this exchange, the more quickly you bite your evil tongue, the better. Your relationships will improve just by you being aware of your actions and intentions, and that alone will have a positive ripple effect.

As you look at the cleanses and clogs of personal relationships, ask yourself what things you're doing that either cleanse or clog them. Consider that everything that comes out of your mouth in a relationship is an opportunity to either cleanse or clog it. Every exchange is an opportunity that will either connect you to or disconnect you from the other person.

CLEANSE	CLOG
Lovingly preparing meals together at home—thereby avoiding both clogging food and spending money to dine out (triple-bonus cleanse!)	Lacking empathy with that person
Spending quality time together	Fault-finding, criticizing, and judging (always pointing out what they did wrong)

Enthusiastically taking the other person's calls (major cleanse—it makes the other person smile inside that you're so happy to hear from them, and it strengthens the relationship)	Maximizing problems
Finding out what the other person needs and giving it to them	Shaming the other for having wants and needs
Validating your partner's life challenges; showing empathy	Focusing more on your needs than theirs
Making a "love list" of what you want from another person and embodying those qualities yourself	Using negative talk with and against that person
Honoring the other person's dreams or goals	Failing to acknowledge—or intentionally ignoring—their efforts to improve or change
Being that person's rock or cheerleader	Expecting too much, or expecting more than your partner can give
Focusing on what you have to offer more than what you're trying to get	Forgetting or failing to validate your partner's needs
Following through with what you say you'll do	Not listening to or hearing what the other person has said
Focusing on what is right about your partner and the relationship	Using sex to manipulate your partner
Being there for your partner during their darkest times	Fostering unhealthy dependencies within relationships

Admittedly, relationships can highlight our stickiest points of communication and vulnerability, and sometimes the most cleansed way of communicating isn't going to create a solid-gold outcome. These tricky situations could be with an ex-husband or wife, a parent, a sibling, a child (adult or otherwise), or even a partner or friend with whom you're in conflict. These are examples of relationships where we choose to cleanse because it will prevent *further* damage in an already-tense situation. In such cases we do what we can to keep things clear, but going forward, my hope is that you can avoid creating more damaging clogs. As you cleanse yourself and connect to your desires, you'll experience easier communication and more joy between you and whoever you're in a relationship with.

FOCUS ON YOU

> *"It's not selfish to love ourselves. It clears us so that we can love ourselves enough to love other people."*
>
> — LOUISE HAY

For all of us, self-care plays an enormous role in whether or not we have enough juice to address life's many tasks. Taking care of everyone else before we address our own needs, wants, and desires—something women especially tend to do—is a surefire way to clog ourselves. That clog disconnects us from both our present experience and our ideal future, and in this day and age, it'd be a shame to siphon off what's good from ourselves because we're so adept at doing what we think we *should*.

Much of the time, the clog in this category is when we are *not* engaging in self-care. We can get into a pattern of not prioritizing our needs, or taking time for ourselves, and we *need to* in order to provide others with the level of care we want to give. In looking at the cleanse or clog lists that follow, know that they're meant to inspire you to think of more ways you can prioritize your self-care, as well as to help you see where you might be inadvertently stifling your own rest, relaxation, and recharging.

CLEANSE	CLOG
Keeping your vessel clean (major cleanse!)	Overeating
Practicing radical self-love	Being a "couch potato"
Celebrating your triumphs, both large and small	Avoiding friends when you're sad
Joining a gratitude club	Ignoring your needs or dismissing any pain or medical issues
Creating a nonnegotiables list of things you won't reschedule, period, such as a bubble bath, time alone to read, exercise, or yoga	Toughing it out in the face of crisis
Going to the doctor or a therapist	Missing checkups and ignoring your symptons for an extended period of time
Getting a massage when you need it—whether it's once a week or twice a year	Getting overwhelmed by bad news in the media
Hiring domestic help and delegating chores to lighten your load	Indulging in negative self-talk (major double-dog clog—it is programming your brain and creating a toxic reality!)
Writing in your journal	Sacrificing your need to have personal time
Making a vision board	Trying to do everything by yourself
Doing daily affirmations	Saying yes when you really mean no
Calling your cheerful friend who will boost you on the frequency scale	Calling your less-than-positive friend on your way home from work and listening to his or her nonstop complaining

More than the big sweeping declarations we make, it's our little everyday habits that change our experience of our life. If we are true to our needs, choosing the cleansed connection with ourselves verses a clogged disconnection, we stand to fare far better in our efforts to increase our overall happiness.

DIAL UP YOUR SPIRITUALITY

*"It is the unseen and the spiritual in [people]
that determines the outward and the actual."*

— THOMAS CARLYLE

It is often difficult to separate spirituality from self-care, as generally they're inextricably linked. Feeling connected to your best self, the *you* that you want to be in the world, can be seen as the by-product of having a solid foundation in self-care and a spiritual practice. By contrast, feeling that disconnection or void between you and your highest expression of love is the easiest way to know you're out of balance or clogged in this area.

See if any of the ideas below resonate with you, since it is in those moments of honesty when you'll be able to unpack an unmet need in this area. Once you are honest about the need, you can move toward meeting it for yourself with more clarity and intention.

CLEANSE	CLOG
Expressing gratitude	Avoiding your spiritual work
Meditating	Clinging to anger, holding grudges, or harboring resentments (major clog)
Going to a house of worship or attending a workshop to help you connect to something bigger than you	Believing what other people think of you is any of your concern

Mindfully doing your daily routines or practicing self-care (major cleanse)	Playing the victim or falling into the blame game
Knowing and living in your purpose	Engaging in gossip or *lashon hara*
Helping others out of kindness and connection; showing generosity and respect to others	Expressing negative self-talk
Praying	Stewing in guilt or shame
Reading books on spirituality or studying something new, like *A Course in Miracles* or the ancient Hawaiian practice of *ho'oponopono*	Making someone else feel guilty

I've said it before in this chapter, and it bears repeating: only you know if you're cleansed and dialed in. Whatever your spiritual connection is, though, I hope it helps you see that we are all one and we're in this together.

SYNCHRONICITIES, MAGIC, AND PROBABILITIES

What I've learned is that when you get your life in balance, the most surprising synchronicities and magic show up as a result. Making small shifts is relatively easy, and it's those shifts over time that change our core programming, since it has so many layers. And in the end, it's so worth it.

My favorite quote from Chazz Palminteri in *A Bronx Tale* is, "The saddest thing in life is wasted talent, and the choices that you make will shape your life forever." Those choices are either connecting you to or disconnecting you from the future you want. And with each choice, your reality and your life's probable outcomes shift . . . every day, in every moment. We can change our probabilities by interrupting our default programming, like sticking a finger in an old frame-by-frame cartoon reel. And even one single choice can—and *does*—affect the outcome of our life.

When Chazz encouraged me that through my writing this book I was going to help a lot of people, I took it to heart. He insisted that keeping my vessel clean was how I would transmit the purity of my message, and I took that idea and ran with it.

When you get yourself out of that 95 percent of your unconscious programming, you'll start to notice the synchronous differences around you. If you choose to do one thing differently on one day, you're going to call new opportunities into your experience.

You'll never know if those new opportunities were there all along or if they appeared because you feel better and you've moved up the frequency scale. But it's in that wake of feeling better, of cleansing your life, of getting to the balance of 80/20, when you experience the synchronicities and magic. As soon as you start moving in the 80 percent cleansed-and-connected direction, you clean out the mud in your wounds that would cause scar tissue if left alone—tissue that would undoubtedly clog you and keep you from taking that one step in the direction of your dreams and desires.

While the experience of them will be different for everyone, synchronicities and magic are attached at the hip, and they are always within each other's grasp. I can't predict what the synchronicities and magic will be for you, but I can predict that they'll be there.

A synchronicity is running into that unexpected person you haven't seen in years (that you were just thinking about). It's listening to that subtle internal voice that tells you to turn left, to call your friend Mindy, or to stop for groceries on the way home. And it's that force that arranges those choices to surprise you with a new piece of information, a new feeling, or more inspiration for whatever it is you need to do next.

What is magic? Magic is when the obstacles seem to melt away. It's when things start happening for you with ease. Magic is when your relationships, circumstances, and struggles start to transform; problems uncharacteristically resolve; and your life becomes easier and more effortless. And as one of my most trusted employees, Roxanne, has said, magic is when "everything just seems to fall into place."

Synchronicities and magic might seem like the results from all this cleansing, but they're just the beginning. Surprisingly, it's the probabilities that have shifted because of your new choices that truly change your life. When you're cleansing and connecting to yourself and others, you'll often experience synchronicities and bursts of magic because you're feeling better. When you feel better, you think better; when you think better, you use words that work; and when you use words that work, you create a better reality for yourself.

EXERCISE: FINDING YOUR CLEANSES AND CLOGS

Now it's your turn. Take your journal and turn it sideways. Make 6 columns, one each for health, finances, career, personal relationships, self-care, and spirituality.

In each category write down 10 habits, recurring thoughts, or behaviors you are aware of. Then, next to each one, write down whether it is a *cleanse* or a *clog*.

Once each column is filled in, evaluate the results. Do you have at least 8 out of 10 items in each column under the cleanse category? Tally your ratios and write them at the top of each column.

It should now be clearer to you which areas in your life are a struggle. Awareness is the first step with any change, so with that let's dive in to the next level.

On another page of your journal, make another list with the changes you're *willing to consider making* in each area that has a ratio of less than 80/20. They don't have to be major changes—and, in fact, I encourage you to start with what feels easiest. What are you willing to do differently to get yourself into the 80/20 ratio? For example, I decided to cancel some of my magazine subscriptions that were cluttering my house.

Don't forget to celebrate your cleanses as well. Every personal win, no matter its size, deserves a little dance break—wouldn't you agree?

(For a deeper look at this exercise, visit MaryShores.com, where you can list all your habits and patterns in each category and we'll do the math for you—as well as help you come up with ideas to rebalance your ratio.)

When it comes to the 80/20–cleanse/clog–connect/disconnect principle, it's important to remember that small changes can and do happen on a moment's notice, but that their larger impact on your life may take longer to see. Lasting change is a practice of patience. Even so, shifting your life from *clog* to *cleanse* is going to be exciting. Your brain, as we've seen, is an organ like none other. It is capable of the most miraculous functions when you let it do its thing. Envision the outcome you want, identify the areas in which you're willing to consider moving from clog to cleanse, take a small step in that direction, and watch as your transformation comes toward you.

In the next chapter, we'll finally explore the promised Do Not Say list, and we'll revisit this chapter's exercises to look for ways the words on the Do Not Say list may be impacting your life—whether you realize it or not.

CHAPTER 6

KNOCK OFF THE NEGATIVE TALK: AND OTHER SAGE ADVICE ABOUT SUCCESS

"Out of your vulnerabilities will come your strength."

— ATTRIBUTED TO SIGMUND FREUD

In this chapter you will learn how your thoughts and words define you. I will teach you how to replace your negative self-talk with affirming positive talk. I will also teach you how to embrace dark emotions and utilize them to move closer to your ideal self.

YOU ARE WHAT YOU THINK

If you had asked me a few years ago to tell you about my life, I would have described it with one word: *hectic*. As a single mom of two boys and the CEO of a growing company, I also prioritized my personal development and learning as well as my health and fitness. To say I felt like I was spread thin would be an understatement, and trying to fit it all in was a constant struggle. In fact, in my rushed and always-running-late lifestyle, I almost fell down an entire flight of stairs. Luckily I caught myself mid-tumble before I got hurt too badly. But it didn't cause me to slow down. Why would it? To me, this was just how life was.

One afternoon at work, I ordered lunch from a restaurant nearby and sat in my office with the door closed, eating quietly and trying to catch my breath from the nonstop barrage of the day. Never one to miss an opportunity to multitask, I opened YouTube on my computer and tuned in to a video about intention. By the time 15 minutes of other videos had autoplayed, I found myself wading in a sea of information I hadn't even known existed just one hour before.

I came across a clip from an educational film called *What the Bleep Do We Know!?* In the short three-minute video, I immediately found myself identifying with the main character, played by Academy Award–winner Marlee Matlin. She's rushing to catch her train (for which she's late). She's irritated and on a tense phone call with someone I assumed was her boss. And, in frustration at both herself and the situation, she half-shouts into the cell phone that she will get there "in ten minutes!" I found myself staring at this woman on the screen, fascinated by how closely our lives seemed to match, even though the circumstances were very different.

Matlin accidentally spills half a medicine bottle's contents across the train platform, and she misses her second train as she's bent over collecting her pills. A knot tightened even more in my stomach as I watched her purse her lips as she picked up her medicine, silently berating herself for making her already hectic day even worse. *This is my life, and I feel this daily frustration too,* I thought.

In the next frame, the character gets distracted for a moment and notices an exhibit a few feet away on the subway platform. The camera pans across a series of pictures in large backlit display cases that capture the results of Dr. Masaru Emoto's water experiments. The exhibit guide explains how Dr. Emoto exposed glasses of water to music, spoken words, typed words, pictures, and video, then froze each sample of water and examined the crystals under a microscope to study the effects of the intentions on the water. The images in the subway exhibit were of those crystals.

I watched in wonder, alongside the actress's character I identified so much with, as we both saw photographic proof that whenever the water was exposed to words like *love, truth,* or *happiness,* or to upbeat, positive music, the frozen water crystals became beautiful, unique, snowflakelike designs. By contrast, whenever the water was exposed to negative words like *hate, rejection,* or *kill,* or to negative or grating music, the crystals formed without any symmetry or beauty and looked haphazardly clumped together.

The exhibit guide's final thought on the presentation highlighted how fascinating it was to consider the implications of Dr. Emoto's water experiments, especially considering that humans are made up of mostly water. With that idea something shifted inside me, and I could literally feel pieces of formerly disconnected information starting to find their way to one another in my brain. Then a stranger leans over to Matlin's character near the exhibit, and as if he was speaking directly to me too, says: "Makes you wonder, doesn't it? If thoughts can do that to water, imagine what our thoughts can do to us."

Although Dr. Emoto's claims have been controversial in the scientific community, many studies have been conducted on the impact of words on the brain. Neuroscientist Dr. Andrew Newberg and professor and well-known researcher Mark Waldman together have extensively researched and written about the connection between words and the brain. In their book *Words Can Change Your Brain,* they write: "A single word has the power to influence the expression of genes that regulate physical and emotional stress."

In the moment that I watched the water-crystal formation in the experiment, it all clicked. It was as if all the information I'd been learning made sense in relation to everything else: *all our life experiences are happening at the level of our cells.* This includes the effect of words on our cellular structure.

I thought about how, over time, repeatedly subjecting ourselves to a toxic environment would literally make us sick. But never before had I understood that our words and thoughts could be responsible for the sickness at the level of our cells.

In the next half hour, I watched the video several more times, each time picking up another bit of information I hadn't seen in the last viewing. Swiftly I found compassion for myself for having gone through the destructive dissolution of my marriage, and I could understand why I was on edge all the time. I'd been hurled the nastiest, cruelest insults by my ex-husband, and being exposed to that for so long had taken its toll on my body, mind, and spirit.

As someone who repeatedly withstood such a stressful and hurtful situation, I not only gained clarity about a few behaviors I knew I wanted to change immediately from seeing this video clip, but it also created an inner momentum. Even though I knew what negative, self-berating, self-deprecating words did to relationships—whether personal or professional—I hadn't ever considered the actual biological repercussions, in either the speaker of the negative words or the hearer. Right then I saw the logic, the biology, and the science behind the effect of disempowering words, and I saw how that language was affecting me, my family, my employees . . . and essentially *everyone* who heard or used the disempowering language. And this new information also gave me insight on what I knew to be true about the brain, which became an invitation for me to take the data I'd studied just for my own curiosity more seriously.

By the time I'd found this video, the Conscious Communications training had already been in full swing for years in my business, and it was also being implemented in a number of other local businesses. But like most inventions, the system had been born out of desperation to solve a problem. It was during the real estate bubble—a few years before the economic collapse of 2008—and no one was interested in hearing about the over-inflated economy or their mounting personal debt. I could no longer convince people who owed money to pay their bills just because it was the "right thing to do." What's more, it seemed that all the other more established debt collector tactics, like intimidation, no longer worked either.

What I observed was that when my employees used negative words, those words themselves zapped the nervous systems of both the employee and the customer on the phone. Whenever anyone heard the word *no* (or any of the other words that eventually found a home on the Do Not Say list), it would automatically trigger their nervous system to react in fight-or-flight. . . and it was most often *fight*. As a business owner, in order to get the outcomes I wanted, I had to find a way to get my staff to be less combative.

I decided to train my staff to focus on the solution, not the problem, instead of arguing about money. The more they said the negative words on the Do Not Say list, the more they would get stuck in a clogged, predictable, negative state of defensiveness. Not only did the old way drive my bottom line into the ground, but it also drained my staff's energy, morale, and enthusiasm. People struggled to want to do their jobs, and I could see how quickly the snowball effect would turn into an avalanche if I didn't turn things around.

I had originally turned to implementing Conscious Communications for two main reasons: 1) because people wouldn't budge to pay their debts, and 2) my staff needed to succeed at their jobs in order to want to do good work and keep coming to the office. Eventually the training became about more than just safeguarding the bottom line. I saw how these negative words reverberated throughout the office and actually dragged my employees into dark emotional states, and I wanted to stop contributing to the problem of incessant negativity and be part of the solution. These people's experiences mattered to me; and I saw the words on the Do Not Say list affecting my family's communication, my friendships, my relationships with others . . . This impacted everything, and the solution to this epidemic of negativity was unfolding organically before me.

Integrating the new information I had learned from Dr. Emoto's water experiment—the science supporting how powerfully negative words impact our biology—I felt incredibly validated that all along there was something else to the system, something much bigger than I'd been teaching. It wasn't just about *say this, get this reaction*. It uncovered the next layer of why the system worked, the aspect of the effect our words have on a cellular level—that what we say really *does* affect our energy (and biology) and that of those around us.

I'll be the first to admit that even though I created this effective system at work, I wasn't always able to merge my professional knowledge with my personal life. As a single mom of two then-preteen boys (one of whom has special needs), I felt reactive much of the time, and could easily snap at my kids if they got out of line. But half the time, I hardly noticed I was reacting in the first place, let alone had the forethought to stop myself before I lashed out.

For me the biggest change that came after understanding the biological connection to disempowering words was that I became much more cautious in how I spoke to my children and to myself. Turns out, when you're thinking twice about what you say to another person because of how it will first affect *your* cells and *your* body, it is much easier to become aware of your behavior and nip outbursts in the bud.

Simply put, words and phrases that keep dialogue open and keep reactiveness at a minimum are along the lines of: *I'm happy to*, *I want to assure you that*, and *I can see your point of view*. This is true in the workplace, in relationships with others, and when we're talking to ourselves.

In short, I saw the larger implications for the Conscious Communications system, as I could now tangibly see how disempowerment impacted our life beyond the fleeting moment of negative thinking or default statements that turn our emotions sour. What's more, disempowering words cause us to do more than just dismiss our true nature, they encourage us to act out of alignment with our deepest desires. All our thoughts and words affect us, and I was beginning to see the ways our words open the doorway for the pattern of negativity to embed itself into our cells.

YOUR WORDS DEFINE YOU

Whether we like it or not, stress is a normal part of life, and I'm not implying that it shouldn't be. There are certain circumstances in life when we expect and tolerate higher levels of stress than other times, like planning a wedding, grieving the death of a loved one, or starting a family. And even though these events can feel overwhelming, we know they're "acute." At some point we'll get a break from the intensity.

In Chapter 3, we talked about how trauma—as well as chronic, intense, and elevated stress—affects the body. Recurring traumas (or their associated thoughts or memories) and chronic stress are responsible for regularly sending messages to the endocrine system to create matching chemical recipes that respond to ongoing or repeated stressful situations. What we haven't talked about yet is that this is how something that might have started out as a string of bad days can easily turn into a string of bad weeks, which can turn into bad months, bad years, and eventually into *I'm just a miserable person.*

With these kinds of near-constant triggers, day in and day out, the chemical recipes in the body associated with the thoughts and feelings of the triggers are elevated for so long that even something as small as the cashier at the grocery store moving too slowly can send us over the edge. When we are regularly flooded with an intense chemical recipe for extended periods of time, eventually the ways we respond to the ordinary situations in our life become reactive. As we talked about in Chapter 2, this is how our knee-jerk responses to things, however unpleasant they are, become our default setting. It's a prime example of how an ongoing challenge changes your behavior. And when that behavior moves swiftly along a highly trafficked neural pathway, it creates what we know of as our subconscious programming.

In other words the body's creation of chemical recipes to match your chronic stress and trauma doesn't affect just your body or your overall health. With time this actually changes your personality. This is how we can decide that our irritability or anger is *just how we are.* Our stressors have in essence hardwired our neural pathways to default to those personality traits. Once our personality is skewed because of our chronic stress or trauma (or both), everything we see will be through that lens— the lens of avidya, misperception. The reticular activating system (RAS) will follow directions and identify evidence to support that *this is just how my life is* mantra, whether that means living in poverty, living with an abusive partner, or living with a draining, exhausting, and unfulfilling job.

It can be easy for us to become addicted to this state of mind, because it becomes our new normal, especially when the words that flood our mind during our consistently stressful experiences are involuntary and disempowering. In this set way of living, any attempts we make to pull ourselves out of this state of mind will feel difficult. This is because our programming, as well as the corresponding memorized chemical recipe, is constantly fighting to put us back at our baseline—even if our baseline feels awful.

HAVING A POVERTY CONSCIOUSNESS

One Halloween I was out to dinner with a small group of friends at a local restaurant. When it came time to order, the waiter asked one of my girlfriends if she wanted something to eat. She waved her hand in the air in front of the closed menu, shook her head, and said, "Too rich for my blood." Though she didn't know it, this statement was an affirmation—a piece of information she was sending to all the cells in her body, as well as to her brain—that gave marching orders to continue living like someone with less than "rich blood" would. My friend's negative affirmation of lack of abundance in her own life told me a lot about how she felt about herself, even if it was an "observable truth" of which she was thoroughly convinced. Her keeping the phrase *too rich for my blood* on standby for occasions like this only encouraged her cycle of struggling, and it also insulted those of us who were eating at that table and didn't share her belief about the food. It was divisive and uncomfortable, and everyone at the table could feel it.

Another example of this kind of negative affirmation is when people say things like *I'm a mess*, or *I could never do that*. When we say these kinds of things, we're often not even aware we're doing it. But it doesn't matter: the words and thoughts still embed the corresponding chemical recipe of *I'm a mess* even farther into our cells, whether we're conscious of it or not.

The involuntary and repetitive things we say about and to ourselves are working against our ultimate desires. There are dedicated neural pathways for involuntary speech, and your chemical recipe and your neural pathways are effective at directing your life in a certain way. Even as recently as six months ago, when I was on a retreat, my friends caught me involuntarily affirming that I was disorganized. Ordinarily I would notice this and would immediately see this as disempowering or negative. This time I hadn't even heard myself. I hadn't realized that my involuntary affirmation of what I saw as the "truth" or "reality" in front of me was keeping me in that self-identified state of disorganization.

Most often we reinforce negative statements about ourselves without even realizing we are doing it. It requires work to catch ourselves when we dish out a default *I am* statement that affirms something we don't want to exist anymore. Yes, it's difficult, but it can be done.

USING THE TOOLS YOU GAIN FROM THE DARKNESS

Before we move on, I'll acknowledge the elephant in the room: none of us wants to look at our darker feelings. In fact, very few people want to think, feel, or experience negativity in any way, as it is genuinely unpleasant to have those feelings. As much as we'd like it to be otherwise, bad things *do* happen, and we often don't want to acknowledge the depth of the pain, or we can't understand why this bad thing or traumatic experience crashed into our life.

Dealing with this type of surprising darkness can be confusing, frustrating, depressing, painful, and infuriating, but it's actually a catalyst for transformation. Here's what I mean: Despite your inclination to rapidly process and move on to a better-feeling thought, you need to let the weariness, grief, anger, rage, or spite *be whatever it needs to be.* You can't pretend that bad things never happen. They do. The solution, as you'll see shortly, is allowing yourself to feel the range of emotions in the aftermath of emotional, draining, or traumatic events. This *is* the process that keeps the emotions flowing through you. Feeling them is what ensures they won't get stuck in your body and cause more problems down the line.

This is preventative self-care. You can't avoid feeling sadness or darkness of any kind, but leaning into the darkness to listen for what it has to tell you is a life skill that grows stronger each time you practice it. By showing your negative emotions the respect they deserve, you redirect yourself from living in a negative state of *being*.

About a year ago, I felt like I was getting depressed. It was winter and I could feel the vitamin D deficiency in my body due to lack of sunshine, but something felt different from typical seasonal depression. I felt overwhelmed with life, my overall energy was noticeably lower, and I was depleted in every way. After a few weeks of this not only persisting but *worsening*, I noticed that it was a deep sadness, and I feared it was becoming a more serious problem. It was beginning to affect my ability to work. All I looked forward to was my cozy bed, and I had stopped reaching out to friends so I could be alone. I felt like I was in a hole. It was dark and scary and somehow I just knew: *this is depression.*

I decided to take control. I had no idea how to get out of the hole I was in, but I knew I wanted out. This was more serious than just a few bad days, or a few challenging weeks. Beyond that I was both blasé and baffled. Knowing as much as I did about the brain, about disempowering words, and about how negative thoughts and words powerfully modify our cells, I held on to my awareness of how important it was to be careful in how I was talking to myself during this dark time. I'd read plenty of research to remind me not to beat myself up with disempowering words, which used to be an easy default for me when I was in an unreasonable emotional state.

My first step to pull myself out of the hole was writing down a list of affirmations, which was simply what I wanted to be true for my life. I then asked myself what else I could do to help myself, and I made sure I was practicing daily gratitude and selecting items from my Zen 10, the exercise to help alleviate stress we learned about in Chapter 3. After a week or two of this activity, the gray refused to lift, so I had to try another tool.

That's when I decided to make a list of everything that was bothering me. Miraculously, the moment I began labeling and naming what was going on in my life, I began to feel the shift. I still call it a miracle, even though neuroscience backs this activity as a reliable way to shift a person's mind-set about a problem. Matthew Lieberman, a professor at UCLA, conducted a study that monitored participants' brain waves while they were showed pictures of angry or fearful faces, and then were showed similar pictures but with the emotion labeled. His research revealed that just the act of labeling emotions decreased participants' negative response. Similarly, labeling your problems will help you feel better about them. I'd known this before, but to see it happening to me in real time made my understanding of it so much more powerful. It felt like someone had tossed me a flashlight, and even though I was still in the hole, now at least I could see.

As I looked at the list of things troubling me, I had an epiphany. *Anyone* would be overwhelmed and depressed with this list of trials going on in their life all at one time. For example, one of the issues was a large, unexpected expense, equivalent to one year's salary. I was devastated about it. And as if the dominoes were lined up perfectly, at the exact time of my unexpected expense, I also lost a significant amount of money on a bad investment. These were just two of the items on my list. That dreadful list went on and on.

As terrible as that list was, it helped me know that my feelings of depression were normal, which in itself helped me to climb the frequency scale and feel a bit better. The next thing I noticed about my list was that about half the items were actual events, like the unexpected expense, and the other half were fear-based emotions that were triggered by the events, like being fearful of losing my financial stability. Seeing this helped me separate fact from fiction—as fears are usually worries based on an event that hasn't yet, and may never, come to pass. That's when I took my list and made two new lists, separating out the real events from my feelings *about* the events.

I could take action on the things on the list that were *event* based, and I could see what things needed emotional processing rather than physical action. This clarity was a tremendous relief, and it brought me up even farther on the frequency scale. For each of the events, I created an action plan for myself. When I was done, it felt like someone had lowered a lifeline—a rope ladder—down to me as I stood in that hole. I know that just having a plan in place caused my brain to focus on the solution instead of the problem, and it allowed for the slow climb up the frequency scale from desperate and depressed to having a tiny, shining glimmer of hope.

Finally I set my lists aside and began reminiscing about my past triumphs. I thought about other times when I'd been in difficult or overwhelming situations and then overcame them, which gave me the courage I needed to climb that rope ladder all the way and get out of the hole. This added courage and determination to my shiny glimmer of hope, and I was rebuilding my strength by the moment. I eventually found a way out of that hole.

The only way I was able to do this was by focusing on a process to search for a solution rather than drowning in my circumstances. I knew my depression was justified by the enormous amount of trials on the list, but I could have easily conferred with the itty-bitty-shitty committee in my head and beat myself up. After all, many of the problems wouldn't have arisen had I made better choices in my past, which would have been an easy default self-berating statement only a few years ago. But going there wouldn't have helped me lean into the emotions, find a solution, or even understand the situation any better; it would have driven me farther down the frequency scale, which would have only made life harder. There was a time in my life when I would chronically tell myself how stupid I was, but I no longer do that. This change was born from the creation of the Do Not Say list.

It's been quite a learning experience, but I no longer choose to fight with myself (or others) over the circumstances of the event, or rather, over *what is*. What I value is process. Process is so important, and once you get yours into place, you will open up some real magic in your life. When you believe that everything is about your circumstances, you'll drown. You'll be unable to see that it's not about your present circumstances as much as it is about the *choices* you make about the circumstances, about what you do going forward. And no matter what, remember that turning the frustration, anger, or darkness on yourself is not a solution. It's a bad habit. And it'll only distract you from experiencing real, lasting change.

I'm telling you about my own imperfections, the depression, dark thoughts, and emotions I witnessed, and the tools I used (and still use) to navigate out of the dark emotions because I believe this experience will help you. Using the tools you have at your disposal to actively seek a less destructive emotion is something I teach in my workshops too. It is in action that we can find our way. Even if the choices we make don't seem to work like we hope they will, I assure you that the alternative—*not* using a tool to stop self-shaming or self-berating—is a surefire way to keep yourself swimming in a cesspool of negativity.

Remember the concept of a feedback loop? Once you're in a loop, stopping it is like pushing a boulder up a hill—it feels nearly impossible. When you have (inevitable) negative experiences, they trigger the chemical recipe to create negative emotions, which trigger negative words, which will generate more negative experiences. To stop that loop, you can't stop the negative experiences or the negative emotions. But you can stop the negative words. This is the invisible key to finding freedom from the darkness.

It may seem that this idea of stopping the negative words strays from acknowledging the impact of our dark emotions. But know that the practice of staying with and allowing ourselves to process the emotional spectrum without abusing ourselves, especially where there is darkness, is just one way to keep ourselves *cleansed* rather than *clogged*. The words you say to and about yourself are the entry point for you to exercise your power in your life. Your words are what can ignite, redirect, stoke, or even put out your own fire.

When you have a recurring experience in your life that triggers old memories and their associated chemical recipes, just being aware of what's happening won't fix the problem. By stopping at the phase of only recognizing how the pattern and belief structures are playing out in your life, you stand to only create more excuses for negative self-talk. The trick is to search for how it feels to sit with what's happening, and to do so in an empowering, solution-oriented way.

You can do this by making an active choice or intention when you are not in a triggering, stressful, or traumatic situation. While choosing to not beat yourself up with words *during* your emotional tailspin is possible in theory, it's unlikely you'll be able to fight an established neural pathway once the chemical recipe has been set in motion. Set the intention in the relaxing moments when you first crawl into bed at night, or when you write and send your gratitude list, sit down for meditation, go for a walk, or take a bath. Think *nonreactive*.

Here is an example of what this intention setting might sound like:

Going forward, I intend to notice whenever I catch myself saying negative, hurtful, or berating things to myself. And whenever I can, I will reframe the verbal self-harm to a less damaging statement.

Here's an example of damaging self-talk, and how to reframe it to still embrace the experience but lose the dramatic self-deprecation:

Damaging self-talk: *I can't believe I opened my dumb mouth and said that! Why would I say something so stupid?*

Reframed: *I am really disappointed in myself. I am going to change. What can I do differently not to put myself in that situation again?*

By doing this you move up the frequency scale of emotions— even if slightly—because it creates some distance between your identity and the mistake. If you think you *are* your mistake, you're less likely to see a possible solution in a similar situation in the future, since you'll be busy fretting about your inherent, fundamental flaws. No one is perfect, but self-flagellation is like dragging an anvil behind you on your journey of healing, and you have the power to cut the ties.

DON'T BE AFRAID OF THE DARK

It's in our nature to resist painful emotions and want them to go away as much as possible. But the solution is actually to welcome or embrace the dark emotions. Secrecy, silence, and judgment feed dark emotions more than we realize.

The most effective way to make those feelings of despair truly go away is to be vulnerable, acknowledge that they're happening within you, process the emotions, accept them, and believe that you won't feel this way forever. If you fall into an emotional hole and can't seem to get out, don't panic. Instead, know you'll get out at the end of the process, so while you're down there, explore what it's like. What do you uncover when you're in the hole? And when you feel like you can't get out, what are the healthy steps you can take that won't dismiss, deny, or devalue your emotions?

Own the experience with a safe friend and process the emotions with them; move your body; or sing empowering songs. These are a few ideas of how movement and forward motion don't negate the experience but open you up to a more thorough healing. In short, facing the darkness within you in this way is a *cleanse*. The clog—which might show up as something like self-medicating with drugs, alcohol, sex, shopping, or anything else in excess—does nothing to release the darkness. Quick fixes and denial only keep the darkness lodged in the cells of your body.

If you're feeling down right now, here's a self-test: Does acknowledging your dark emotions make you feel exposed? Make a list of things you would never want to tell anyone—not even your best friend. You may never share these darker, vulnerable things with anyone, but I challenge you to sit with the list. Be present with the discomfort on the list. You might not want to shout it from a mountaintop, but denying your darker feelings makes them bounce back up and smack you in the face. When you acknowledge and own your darker feelings, you stop running from them. The silver lining is that when you look at them straight on, they are easier to see than in the sidelong avoidance dance we all do.

Despair is a remarkably powerful emotion. Instead of sinking farther into despair, use it as a tool to remind you of where you *never* want to be again. Think of it like this: Despair is the flattest emotion a human can experience. If nothing else, when you're in that place, you know that you don't want to be there forever (or even for another five minutes, if you can help it). Knowing what you don't want helps you figure out what you *do want*. Painful experiences create catalysts for transformation. Use them as springboards into the life you want.

THE DO NOT SAY LIST

As you read earlier in the chapter, around the years 2004 to 2006, I took notice of some seemingly imperceptible shifts in the economy that I just knew were going to breed a nationwide financial disaster. On the surface it seemed that the economy was thriving, that the American dream was finally attainable for almost everyone. In fact, all anyone had to do to qualify for a mortgage was have a pulse and a credit score above 500. Over the course of about a year, I observed that the spike in overall happiness of Americans seemed to coincide with a decline in the number of Americans who were willing to pay their bills. This made being the CEO of a collection agency the challenge of a lifetime, so I rolled up my sleeves and looked at it as an opportunity for me to reevaluate our approach. That was when the Do Not Say list was born, which would grow into the full Conscious Communications system.

At its core the Do Not Say list suggests that you stop broadcasting to the world what you don't want, and start talking about what you do want. By default you're going to be affirming something, so why not affirm the experience you want to have instead of the one you want to avoid?

Imagine your negative words and thoughts are a dripping faucet. Just turning the handle tighter isn't going to shut the leak off. You have to go to the water main and shut the valve off, and then fix the faucet. Purposely using empowering words and not allowing yourself to use disempowering words is how you reroute that water away from the involuntary dripping of negativity and toward the voluntary clean and clear flow of personal empowerment.

Saying things like *too rich for my blood*, or *I always do that*, or *this always happens to me* are those insidious, involuntary statements that we don't necessarily recognize. Instead of wasting time sifting through all your default disempowering language, the quicker way to cut off the source of negative and disempowering thoughts and language is through immersion.

What I mean by immersion is filling yourself up with language that is empowering. We'll talk in more detail about the mechanics of how to do this in the next chapter, but the important thing to note is that it is easier and faster to replace disempowering, involuntary statements with new empowering statements instead of taking the time to analyze the history of your disempowering language.

So far everything in this book has explained the *why* of your woes. Going forward we're getting into the mechanics of *how* to confront your woes and turn them into *whoas!* These are the *how-to* tools to break through your personal barriers and understand, at a deep level, both how your mind works *and* how you can alter it.

A lot of times, I see friends go on and on about aspects of their lives that aren't working for them, or about why they haven't achieved or accomplished their goals. This is focused on scarcity. It's natural to want to talk about what's not working, as it doesn't take much imagination: *all the good men are taken, there are no good jobs, the economy sucks, the school systems are broken, the food situation in this country is dire,* and so on. By giving our attention to this, we train our inner GPS, or RAS, to look for and identify these realities at every opportunity.

The idea of the Do Not Say list is to give us a tool to help control the things that are coming out of our mouths—both involuntarily and voluntarily. We can then figure out where the red flags are, and think about how we can replace them with the good stuff. It's like going to a spa and doing a weeklong detox cleanse, and then going to another spa to replenish the nutrients you need.

Cleanse yourself from the disempowering talk, and from here forward, we'll focus on filling you back up with the thoughts, words, and behaviors that empower you to live your greatness.

EXERCISE: YOUR DO NOT SAY LIST

With your journal in hand, sit quietly in a place where you can have five to ten minutes without interruptions. Once situated, ask yourself, *What are disempowering words or phrases that do not serve me?*, and write down your answers.

Now look over what you've written down. With your journal in hand sit quietly . . . do not serve me?, and write down your answers. On that list, what are you committed to *never saying about yourself ever again?*

At my company our Do Not Say list evolved over the years, and yours will too. When you're focused on cleansing your life of disempowering speech, you'll more naturally notice when a new word shows up that needs to get added to *the list* and then take the action to put it on there. This simple act is incredibly freeing, and it paves the way for the next stage of life creation we're about to take on.

Whenever you make a statement about yourself, you're creating a chemical recipe in your body that matches the statement—whether good or bad. These hormones actually change your body language, the expression on your face, and even your perception of reality. Knowing that, consider this: how does it benefit you to affirm a reality you don't want to expand? You literally shift your experience of reality through the lens you've established—which starts with the words you say about yourself, to yourself, and to others.

It is important to make a clear decision about the words you are committed to *no longer saying*. And when you catch yourself saying them, gently tell yourself to stop. Do not self-berate. Do not criticize, lament, or judge. Just redirect your thoughts back to where your desired focus is. This is where all the goodness lines up at once: the synchronicities, the magic, and the sweeping probabilities. You'll think, feel, move, speak, and live out a different probability, just by welcoming whatever emotions arise for you without chastising yourself for them.

In short, we are what we say we are. And even though most of us are wrapped up in messages we tell ourselves—messages we're not even aware of—that make saying a positive thing about ourselves feel like a lie, this work changes all that old programming.

In this chapter we learned about the staggering power of words and their ability to bring about both negative and positive change. In the next chapter, we will take this a step further. We will learn to recognize our true self, discovering how to fully step into the person we want to be—the person who we *already are.*

CHAPTER 7

BECOMING WHO YOU REALLY ARE

*"Often, it's not about becoming a new person, but
becoming the person you were meant to be, and already
are, but don't know how to be."*

— HEATH L. BUCKMASTER

We each have a hero or a heroine, someone we look up to—it could be our grandmother, a character from a book, a celebrity, anyone. We each have someone we want to be like, an alter ego. This chapter will help you uncover who that person is, and teach you how to use that alter ego to create a better version of yourself. We will also begin cleaning out the things that are cluttering your life so you can make room for new experiences.

KARMIC DEBT COLLECTING

I've always been intensely curious about the world, but about five years ago—after the fog cleared from my divorce—I found that my desire to understand the nature of the universe had turned itself inward. It wasn't out of some virtuous ambition that I wanted to know myself more deeply; it came after years of studying, struggling, and surviving. It was as if one day I woke up and realized that the pursuit of enlightenment had been with me all along, but now I was finally able to see it.

There was only one problem.

I owned and operated a collection agency. I couldn't think of any other legal job on the planet that was in greater opposition to the path of seeking enlightenment. And no matter how I tried, I couldn't reconcile the two. So much so that it seemed to be all I could read about, seek guidance about from mentors, and write about in my journal. The question of how I would (or even *could*) do both—keep my company *and* seek enlightenment at the same time—seemed to play like a quiet soundtrack that underscored all my interactions, friendships, and life choices.

Months charged forward as I felt conflicted, wondering which of the two selves I'd be forced to abandon. I couldn't see myself surviving or supporting my children without my business, but I also couldn't accept the reality that in order to put food on the table and keep my business open, I had to ignore my desire to seek enlightenment.

This inner conflict carried me from the end of 2012 into 2013, when I went to the Omega Institute and had a chance conversation with a woman I had just met—let's call her Christine. We got to talking, and when she asked me what I did for a living, I tried to force a grin.

"I own and operate a collection agency," I said as plainly as possible. Even though I had confusion about the intersection of work and spirit, I also knew the power of words, and I wanted to keep mine as genuine as possible.

She didn't pry, and I relaxed more and more. It wasn't long before we were talking about what we wanted to experience or manifest in our lives.

That was when I told her about my Magic 8, which is my dream list—big, bucket list–type desires—that I mentioned earlier. During this conversation I mentioned that enlightenment was one of the things on my Magic 8, but that I was worried that seeking enlightenment would interfere or conflict with my business. In a moment of true transparency with a person I felt comfortable with, I shared my big fear: that I would have to give up one or the other.

"How can I merge my paths? How can I pursue an authentic, spiritually driven life, like Marianne Williamson, *and* still be a debt collector, my spirited Julia Sugarbaker self?" I asked. In another few sentences, I explained that my company wasn't a normal collection agency, as far as stereotypes went—that my mission of wanting people to feel good about paying their debts was what I focused on during this time. But the contrast still bothered me.

I didn't expect her answer to be so quick or so clear. I remember Christine leaned toward me just a bit, and my breath caught a little as she told me that she could see that what my company did was *deeply* spiritual.

For a second I thought she was kidding, but there was no humor in her face.

Christine explained that carrying debt isn't just monetary; it's karmic. It represents karmic imbalance; it's an anchor to remind us of our former choices. But eliminating debt? That's clearing all that heavy karma. She pointed out that it could even be karmic clearing from other lifetimes too. I knew there was something to this, because I'd often helped people see the bigger picture of debt. Sure, if you owe money, it weighs heavily on your life. But if anyone has ever owed you money, you understand how that is a burden also.

Here I was looking for ways to link my profession to my deeply personal search for enlightenment, and within minutes of sitting down with this woman I had just met, I was gifted with the awareness that I already had the ability to build a bridge across the divide I felt inside me.

As we spoke Christine helped me to understand that by helping clear other people's karmic debt, I'm helping them live more active, creative, full lives. People who carry debt don't just owe money to a bunch of places, the way it looks on paper. I have seen that they also carry a heavy psychological burden. I realized that

I'm relieving them of that, freeing them up—and that doing this work actually clears my own karma too.

Just like that, the barrier between these two parts of me dissolved, and a bridge was made, easily and effortlessly. Christine put words to what had been going on in my business for years by this point, but it went beyond that. I finally understood—and completely accepted—how my role as a debt collector could be part of the universe's rebalancing, and how important it would be for me to stay focused in my business while remaining on the path to seek enlightenment. This wasn't just a way to reconcile my inner conflict. It was a way for me to live more authentically as myself.

FRIED GREEN AUTHENTICITY

In 1991 the film *Fried Green Tomatoes* hit theaters, and it wasn't long before it became an iconic pop-culture classic. In the movie the character Evelyn, played by Kathy Bates, undergoes a radical transformation that is nothing short of breathtaking.

When we meet Evelyn, nothing about her life seems to be created by conscious design. She's overweight, sedentary, resentful, and stuck in the routine of attending women's meetings with ladies she doesn't like all that much in order to save her marriage to a man who doesn't seem to care. She has no personal power, control, or sense of adventure, and she is so accustomed to letting people treat her poorly that she effectively co-signs their mistreatment with her apathy.

Then Evelyn learns about the power of *Towanda*—an unexplained word used as a battle cry in a tale about personal empowerment—and it impacts her so much that she adopts the word for herself too. In fact, it's not long before the word *Towanda* becomes the name of Evelyn's alter ego, and when she shows up for her life with Towanda's sass and courage, she is unstoppable. She starts exercising, stops eating junk food, stops attending the women's meetings, and starts a career selling cosmetics, all in the name of leaning into a greater sense of independence and reclaiming her identity. Evelyn/Towanda becomes so motivated to take her life back that her dedication to her transformation, coupled with her willingness to detach from any situation or relationship that doesn't support her growth, creates the perfect catalyst to skyrocket her into quickly integrating the different parts of herself, her desires, and her personality.

In the span of the movie, Evelyn shifts from a passive, unhappy, unfulfilled, and uninspired woman to one who embraces her life with enthusiasm and authenticity, eventually merging her alter ego, Towanda, with her day-to-day Evelyn self. In short, she found the thread and followed it, and it led her directly to her authentic self, which is the embodiment of a fully integrated and clearly envisioned sense of identity.

I will help you find yours too.

WHAT WOULD TOWANDA DO!

Before you can begin to identify the core of your own authenticity, you have to know yourself. The core of what I'm teaching you here is to come out and be who you really are, what you really are, and how to step into being that person. When you Decide to—with a big *D*—you can be *anybody* you want to be.

You can't clean your house without first seeing the dirt. Look honestly at your present situation and then see how things could be different. Evelyn needed to see her own life through a new lens before she could embrace Towanda. And just like Evelyn/Towanda, you too get to Decide who you want to be. I imagine that if she could have, Evelyn might have worn a WWTD (What Would Towanda Do?) bracelet as a reminder that she'd already named the way of being that was more in line with her authentic self, and she should dare to dip her toes in the waters of that desire.

We can't all have a wearable reminder to check our choices against the more empowered version of ourselves, though it's not a bad idea. I say this because I've seen so many inspired people gain awareness of who they want to be, set their sails, and stay in the harbor. This happens when, in our mind's eye, we can't see or feel the more archetypal characteristics, traits, quirks, or wit of our authentic self, for example. Making a split-second decision becomes easier and more exciting when we can easily ask ourselves, *WWTD?*

When I speak to groups on this topic, I find that just like I was conflicted with the two life paths that seemed to go in opposite directions—my Evelyn vs. Towanda period—most people have experience with these kinds of conflicting desires or dreams. We are conditioned by our families, friends, and society as to what's "appropriate." But sometimes we realize that our desires have shifted or expanded, and they might look like they're in conflict with what we think is "right." That conflict is what makes our dreams feel irreconcilable with who we are.

By now you must realize that's not even a little true.

When you step into who you really are, it's monumental. Every part of you is important and full of possibilities; if that weren't the case, those desires that seem like they're at odds with each other wouldn't be there . . . but they are.

Have you ever asked yourself what you'd be doing with your life if money weren't an object? It's a question that requires you to be blatantly honest about who you are and what you want. And then commit to one step in that direction, for however many steps it takes, to get closer to that dream.

We are all told that we need to live our life a certain way— *believe this, believe that, be a mother, be a wife, be a success,* and so on, forever. But that way of life may be in conflict with who you really are. Regardless of what the rest of the world tells you, the only way to be completely fulfilled on a daily basis is to allow the real you to live in this world. *Welcome* the real you; get to know yourself and your desires. Look to characters or personality archetypes that you admire, and use them as inspiration whenever you're confronted with the challenge of stepping more fully into who you really are.

Look at it this way: if I can be a successful businesswoman and debt collector while also actively seeking enlightenment, *anyone* can find the intersection of their desires or paths in a way that feels authentic to them. It all comes down to knowing what it is, and who it is, you want to be and embody. When you understand that, you'll be able to find the most authentic version of you—the one that feels like solid ground.

The question *How can a person get to know who they are?* comes up often enough that I've put together a short list of self-exploration questions that should help you feel like you're getting clarity on the basics of you. From there you'll be able to see the basics of where—and who—you'd like to grow toward.

- Where are your food boundaries? What won't you try, and why? And what's on the curiosity list?

- What movies inspire you? What movies make you laugh?

- Do you prefer the sleek architecture of a modern cityscape, or watching the wind move through the trees when the seasons change? Or a blend of both?

- What moves you deeply?

- How do you like your eggs? How do you *not* like your eggs? (Like Julia Roberts in the movie *Runaway Bride,* we can start to embrace who we are when we learn who we are, even down to the scramble—or not—of our eggs.)

- What causes do you find yourself drawn to? From social justice to the environment, from scientific research to emergency relief in developing countries . . . or anything in between. Where do you feel a pull toward advocacy or activism? Have you ever responded to the pull? Why or why not?

- Who are your favorite archetypes, both male and female? Make a list of the qualities you love about them.

As you know by now, there are no wrong answers here, even if what you uncover isn't the version of you that you want interacting with the world as your personal representative.

For now the most important concept is that you begin to get to know who and where you are today, which will set you up to explore the different ways you can move closer to where (and who) you want to be.

CHOOSING YOUR TOWANDA

When we tap in to the collective cultural conversation about who different individuals admire, we find that for the most part we can't agree on much. Who you look up to is different than who I look up to or aspire to be more like, and that's the way it should be.

However, that's not true in every area, and I hope it never will be. What I've noticed is that we *can* all pretty much agree that superheroes are super-awesome, and that having a superhuman trait of some kind would be pretty great. Children get to have these superheroes as aspirational icons, but as we grow up we tend to get "realistic" about who we want to be more like.

It's easier to default to admiring the celebrity, the athlete, or the guru who appears to have what we want. Ask yourself, *Is that really what I want to be more like?*

When I first learned about the value of having a fully formed vision or archetype (or two or three) to use as a guiding light to illuminate the path to my growth, I immediately knew which characters from pop culture I identified with most already, as well as which ones had traits I knew I wanted to further develop.

Like so many of the women I've met or spoken to throughout the years, when I first saw *Gone with the Wind,* I fell in love. I can't remember exactly how old I was when it happened, but the day my eyes first fell on the glamorous Scarlett O'Hara, I identified her as a prime example of who and how I wanted to be—she was the perfect archetype for my developing sense of being a woman, though I didn't use the term *archetype* back then.

Scarlett was an immovable force. She always knew what she wanted, she was business-brilliant, and to top it all off, she was a beautiful, aristocratic seductress too. She was strong and powerful, and it was clear that she was really good at being her most authentic self at all times.

As time passed I held on to the vision of Scarlett O'Hara as a cultural archetype I identified with, and I wanted to be more like her. Her "force to be reckoned with" style was a similarity I saw between us. But still, something didn't quite sit right about using Scarlett as my sole cultural or character archetype. For many years, though, I couldn't quite pinpoint the qualities of Scarlett that I'd outgrown.

Like me, Scarlett was street-smart, business savvy, great with people, and full of wisdom, but when I looked closer at how she had acquired these skills, I realized it was because she was always fighting or struggling. Scarlett was always dealing with a level-10 emergency: her father dies, her daughter dies, there's always a crisis with Rhett, she gets stuck in a fire during the war, she has to escape with Melanie . . . and the list of tragic events goes on. Sure, she holds it together, but with Scarlett there was always something in her life to overcome. It was exhausting just to think about.

I realized that I was done with that fight, that struggle. I didn't want to be strong for everyone else. I wanted relief. I wanted unconditional love and support, not respect, admiration, and a "you've got this" attagirl from afar. It was with that realization that I knew it was time to rethink my cultural archetype.

Enter Dorothy from *The Wizard of Oz*.

When I think about Dorothy, I see a girl who, all along, has had the power within her to change the world. When Dorothy is in trouble of any kind, if she can simply remember to click her heels, she can experience relief from whatever chaos she's walked into. Even with this untapped knowledge and power, throughout her journey she also has the unconditional love and support of the Tin Man, the Scarecrow, the Cowardly Lion, and her little dog, Toto, too. In the most disarming fashion, Dorothy has a way of bringing out the best in people . . . including even the Wizard himself.

I loved this new idea of using Dorothy as my cultural character archetype. Especially when I realized that when Dorothy wakes up, she experiences a miracle—a simple shift in perception to recognize that all the characters in her dream were actually loved ones in her life who have supported her unconditionally all along. I didn't have to totally dethrone Scarlett; she still provided value to me when it came to couth, poise, and command. But the blend of these two feminine energies was and is more in line with where I need to spend my focus.

When I adjusted who I chose as my character archetype, my blinders came off and I could see that the love and support I'd so desperately craved had been around me all along. Just like Dorothy has that light-bulb moment at the end of *The Wizard of Oz*, I also realized my own power to create my whole world. This realization makes letting go of my barrier beliefs that much easier, and having personal archetypes becomes another angle for a workaround. If I find myself struggling, I'll think of Dorothy or Scarlett, and instead of dwelling on how *I* can't figure something out, I'll ask myself, *How would Dorothy or Scarlett handle this?* (My own personal WWDD or WWSD moment.) And from there, I ask myself, *Well then, how can I?*

If we want to stand a chance at creating and living the life we imagine for ourselves, we've got to begin with an authentic understanding of who we are, where we are, and where we want to go. Authenticity is the glue that holds the puzzle pieces of our life's vision together.

GET TO KNOW YOURSELF

A few weeks ago when I was deep in the research to prepare for this chapter, I thought a good deal about the concept of detachment, which simply refers to removing yourself from behaviors or situations that don't line up with what you want.

For example, consider this mini-test:

- Do you want to take a spiritual path, but find yourself watching endless hours of *The Bachelor*? Do you easily get swept into drama or the party scene as your go-to stress relievers or decompression techniques? Can you see how even though these are justifiable actions, they aren't in alignment with your declared desire of being on a spiritual path?

- Or are you someone who's said you want to diet, but you find yourself in the McDonald's drive-through without realizing it until it's too late?

The concept of detaching from behaviors that aren't in alignment with what we want is simple, especially when we see the misalignment in others. On the other hand, when we ourselves are struggling with the alignment, it's not always so obvious.

Just like knocking off the negative self-talk in order to get you closer to a life that resembles the one in your vision, detachment is about knocking off the same kind of self-inflicted future-blocking actions and behaviors. Whether or not this makes complete sense to you, by now you should be willing to look more closely at how your actions line up with what you say you want for your life.

Here are a few more questions to ask yourself:

- *If I were someone other than who I think I am, who would I be?*

- *If I could be anybody, who would I be?*

- *If I were not being what others (including society) prescribed, who would I be?*

- *Am I sacrificing my end-result goals for short-term satisfaction?*

- *What would I change my name to if I could?*

When you know who you are, you will create a life very different than the one you have now. The job is to get in sync with this new identity. When you put your alter ego in charge, your choices will change.

We are taught that the right behavior or circumstances will make us happy. We adopt sayings like: *I will be happy when I have the right house, I will be happy when I have the right partner,* or *I will be happy when I have the right job . . .*

I know it's easier said than done, but what if, as an experiment, you tried to be happy just by becoming who you really are? Just living it and stepping into it?

To get to who you really are, you have to shed layer after layer of who you've been pretending to be; layers of the person that you know, deep down, you are *not*. You're shedding layers of your problems, layers of self-judgment, layers of how others have judged you. Shedding layers of unworthiness, fear, worry, and unnecessary responsibilities. And layers of beliefs and challenges around what other people think you are, or even worse, think you *should* be.

Make choices that resonate with who you are. Live in sync with your true self. Choose a character archetype to guide you, because taking action, big or small, has an impact. And you'll want the impact to point you right in the direction of your dreams.

Through all this my goal in this chapter is to get to the true you, without the layers of the barrier beliefs, unworthiness, judgment, criticism, and challenges others make to your authentic self. When you do this shedding, you can move forward by taking action—and not just any action, the *right* action.

When you are living authentically, when you are being who you really are, you are living on solid ground. When you are holding firm in the center of your truth, you cannot be toppled. In that space, you can step into your best ideas, and you will naturally begin to detach from obligations that will knock you out of sync with your biggest desires. It's a ripple effect, but it starts with moving the tiniest pebble of the best version of you from backstage to center stage.

At the heart of detaching from what doesn't work for you anymore is a very simple (and important) question you should ask yourself:

What's the worst that can happen?

NAME IT, AFFIRM IT, CLAIM IT

If you're living in the rat race and are working on living 100 percent in alignment with your desires and what you really want, chances are that the "worst" thing that will happen as a result of turning down an invitation to something that's not a good fit for you—whether it's for a dinner date or a marriage proposal—is a temporary state of discomfort. It's simply a matter of your willingness to live with the short-term squirm in order to make space—physically, emotionally, and psychologically—for your long-term, end-result goal.

A friend of mine, Rocky, is a great example of how detachment from what doesn't line up with your personal vision can transform every aspect of your life. Rocky was fully immersed in the rat race. He had big dreams for his life but often worked more than 100 hours each week, which barely even allowed him enough time to sleep and shower, let alone anything else.

Rocky's most important value was (and is) freedom, so he deeply resonated with Mel Gibson's character in the film *Braveheart*, in that well-known "Freedom!" scene. As Rocky says, it wasn't until he put "Braveheart Rocky" in charge that he was able to really take his life back and design it as he wanted it to be. He went from working 100 hours a week at a physically challenging, unfulfilling job alongside crews with toxic attitudes to moving down to the Florida sunshine, owning his own business in an industry he's passionate about, mentoring and teaching others, and following his inner GPS.

It's important to remember that when we are in the middle of the detachment process, sifting through our choices to make sure we only say yes to what absolutely works, feeling discomfort is normal. It's a marker of having outgrown what used to work for us. And here's the thing: You will always have problems and obstacles in your life, because *that's life*. You will have obstacles both on the path that you don't want to be on *and* on the path that you do. So you might as well be on the path you want! When Victoria, my friend from my gratitude group, left her corporate life and moved to a commune—which absolutely was on her path and was a step she wanted to take—she discovered that, actually, she didn't want to live in a commune. It was disorganized and inefficient and just not for her. Now, she could have given up and gone back to working at Yahoo . . . but she didn't. She wanted to stay on her spiritual path, but in a way that was right for her. She did a little soul-searching, and now she's pursuing her master's in environmental law, using her gifts to make a change in the world. She told me that when she made the choice to do that, to work on something that used her strengths but that would also make the world a better place, she felt it as a full-body excitement, a sense of complete congruency and clarity. She couldn't *not* do this work.

This is not to say that it's easy to find your true path. In fact, problems and obstacles that you encounter when you're first stepping onto your path can feel *more* uncomfortable. This is because they are new and because now that you are on your path, it feels like these obstacles matter so much more than before. Remember that your gifts will guide you through the difficulties, and you will meet your challenges with greater strength and resilience because you know that you are steadily moving toward where you want to be.

You'll soon see that the more you do this kind of intentional work, the more excited you'll get about what life is bringing you. More reasons to say yes to alignment with your authenticity makes the *no thank you* response easier to live with, because eventually those options won't hold the same appeal they did before. The more active you are in detaching from what doesn't work for you in favor of what does, the better you'll feel. The intensity and frequency of those moments of discomfort will become so unfamiliar that when you do have one, it will only be a tiny blip on the radar of your awesome day.

When you lose your attachment to who you thought you should be, your life will go through a transition. You *will* change. Just as a snake sheds its old skin to grow a new one, you're shedding the old you to make room for the new life. It can be incredible, and it can also be excruciating and everything in between.

I realize how simple it sounds, but the simple way isn't always the easy way. In my view this process is the most effective way to go about change, but it does require patience. I've seen it take years before a person finally feels comfortable enough with themselves to accept only the best for themselves, while declining and/or rejecting anything less.

Completely dedicate yourself to the newly minted version of you, and see it as an adventure worth taking, because detachment from your old behaviors is *so important* if you want to begin taking steps in a new direction. If you can commit to this, celebrating even small, consistent wins, you can supercharge your results.

Regular dedication to the new behaviors and choices is what reinforces all your new core beliefs, and when you're reinforcing these new neural pathways, all your new efforts will begin to stick. You've done all this work to figure out who you want to be, and this alter ego will help usher you into a more integrated and confident version of you. Turning away from what doesn't work for you will create space for you to attract new experiences, relationships, and opportunities. Be willing to say yes only to what lines up with the newly cultivated vision of yourself. If it doesn't fit the updated definition of who you want to be, it doesn't get to stay.

Most people go their entire lives thinking that their present situation is "good enough" to get by, holding to the belief that they "can't complain" or they "should be grateful." These people live from one disappointment to another, settling for the job, the house, the partner, or the parts of their personality that don't feel totally right, but they don't know exactly what's out of sync. When these aspects of their lives meet *just enough* needs to "get by," but not enough to truly fulfill their desires, their "good enough" becomes another justification to sacrifice long-term desires for short-term satisfaction. Don't let your dreams, no matter how big or small they seem in the moment, settle in the realm of "good enough."

Do the work of exploring what you really want. Name it, affirm it, claim it as though it's already true, and then release yourself from what's keeping you from it. Then begin the practice of turning away from the behaviors that don't work for you any-more. Ask yourself:

- *What do I need to let go of?*
- *What's unimportant now that I am holding on to?*
- *What am I most skillful and talented at?*
- *How can I step in that direction and turn away from the old?*

The simple act of graciously saying no to what is draining you will naturally make room for more opportunities to pour in. It's the way the universe works.

You're in the active energy of trending in the direction of your authenticity now. You have your character archetype as a guide to help you stay present and keep checking in with what feels right moment to moment. Because of this, it'll get easier to see and accept the choices, behaviors, and invitations in your life that help you fulfill your dreams. All choices point you back to yourself.

SPRING-CLEAN YOUR LIFE

Each year in the springtime, it's pretty common to hear peo-ple's updates of how dramatic or uneventful their spring-cleaning ritual is. For whatever reason when the earth cycles into spring and begins to blossom with new life, we feel the need to purge and clean. Whether it's a cultural concept or a biological impera-tive, we tend to make space for the new at the beginning of spring.

It seems probable that without the collective push to purge during this season, our closets may very well be bursting, unclose-able, and full of stuff we wouldn't even remember getting as a gift or buying for ourselves. There's a valuable lesson in this annual tradition, and we could stand to apply it in other areas too.

For a moment imagine going shopping for a new spring and summer wardrobe right around the time when the flowers first bloom. Pretend you've splurged on a new outfit or two (or more)

and you feel so great in your new clothes that you can't wait to get home, hang them up, and get dressed up for a night on the town.

Now imagine that even though you've just bought some beautiful new clothes, you haven't taken the time to spring-clean (or *any* time to clean or purge those closets, for that matter), and there's no room in your home for your new outfits—the ones you felt so sharp wearing. No matter what temporary solution you might think up in the moment to keep your new clothes looking nice, it doesn't solve the bigger problem, which is that a cluttered house signals that there's no room for the new, even if the old is broken, ill-fitting, or outdated.

Think of your mind as the house for your thoughts. If your mind is cluttered, the lens of your perception will reflect that. Decluttering clears that avidya, allowing fresh ideas, insights, and opportunities to come to you. However, if a cluttered mind is your point of creation, what kind of mess will you bring into being? How could you expect to create a fulfilling circumstance without first purging the space of what no longer fits?

In short, if your mind is a mess, your life will reflect that mess.

Your mind is the hoarder of all your beliefs, and whatever other things it's storing, whether needed or not. It's painful for hoarders to rehabilitate themselves, and it's a similar struggle when you try to rid the mind of clutter.

In many cases we don't even know the mind-clutter is there, but we hold on to it because it's familiar. When your behaviors are conniving and strategizing, your energy gets directed into triage rather than creation. It is diverted to fixing problems, and this winds up being a big expenditure of energy—energy that could be used to create instead.

What things have you been doing that have nothing to do with being your own Dorothy, Scarlett, Braveheart, or Towanda?

A cluttered mind clogs your ability to see what's possible. Don't you want to give yourself room for the full exploration of what's possible?

THE MAGIC OF DECLUTTERING

When you begin to live in authenticity, you naturally make better choices, which—also naturally—declutters your mind. A clear mind attracts less drama, which also gives you the space to create whatever you desire. In *Fried Green Tomatoes,* Evelyn transforms her life by removing bad habits, negative self-talk, and negative self-treatment, but she doesn't stop there. She takes her power back by earning her own income, by proudly owning her identity and self-worth. And through all of it, it's implied that she's cleared out the old, outmoded operating system and has made space in her brain for new ideas to come in. She spring-cleaned her life.

What we didn't see, though, is Evelyn undertaking a complicated decluttering process in order to have her freedom. It was quite the opposite, actually. The detachment and repositioning process is what naturally kick-started the clearing and decluttering, and it opened up space for Evelyn's innovation and creativity, just as it will for you. This is a natural part of the journey. Decluttering is much easier when you're in the action of repositioning yourself and re-creating your authentic self.

When you declutter your mind, getting the coordinates of where you are in alignment with where you're heading, the by-product is a tidier physical space, a clean slate to create, and an open source of ingenuity for smoother problem-solving. When you manifest and create from *that* mind-set, it completely changes what you have the capacity to create.

But here's the best facet of the entire process: the decluttering experience itself is a by-product, not a process in itself.

Decluttering happens when you are dedicated to detaching from the old and stepping into the new. It's simply an element of keeping your vessel clean, and it's another way I like to describe getting your thoughts, feelings, words, and actions into alignment so you can skyrocket yourself more quickly toward your desires.

If you've been doing the self-discovery work throughout this book so far and have begun pivoting away from what's not in sync with your authenticity in favor of what is, you're inevitably going to notice the open real estate in your brain, or spare "brain change," as I fondly call it. All that clutter, negotiating, self-deprecating thinking, and negative self-talk takes up tons of mental energy without you even realizing it.

The simplest way to explain this is to think of the mental energy you have in a day as your mental bank account, and every day before you wake up, you get an automatic deposit of 100 units of mental energy. Each thought and unit of speech you allow yourself to linger on—anything you give credence, energy, affirmation, or confirmation to—you should consider a deduction in your brain change, or a deduction from the units of mental energy you have reserved for that day. Have you noticed that there are days when—and you aren't even sure how—by noon, you're totally depleted of mental units of energy? This can show up in so many different ways, from feeling angry to aggressive driving, to yelling at your partner, kids, or friends.

Sometimes this happens because we are so depleted over time that we haven't given ourselves the space to recharge our mental reserves. Other times it happens because an event or circumstance can be so taxing that it takes everything we have and leaves us with nothing but mental and emotional fumes—and an unwavering desire for a nap.

This is just like how you would budget the money you'd spend if you were planning a nice evening out or a vacation. Making conscious choices about how you'll allot your brain change—your mental energy stores throughout the day—is simply a natural part of being a functional adult.

Once you've identified your desires, articulated them, and embarked on your explorative journey toward more authenticity, you'll find that your reserves won't deplete themselves nearly as quickly, and certainly not without your express permission.

The act of detachment will lead you to clear out all the mental clutter and whatever else is keeping you out of sync with what you really want. We need to disassemble the old personality traits that are boulder-sized hurdles between you and your desires, and assemble new, more functional traits that are lined up with your personal definition of authenticity.

As you might imagine, when you're living your truest, most authentic self and are willing to detach and reposition yourself from what's *not* in alignment, a natural by-product is a loosening of the grip your old barrier beliefs have held on you.

In simple terms doing the work in this chapter—and this entire book so far—will make it that much easier to realize what is no longer your truth. The processes I've presented to you allow you to embrace this learning the easy way—through observation and awareness—rather than stumbling into confusion, heartache, and costly mistakes that steal more of your present moments.

You'll have a sense of clarity about your decisions. There will be no way to misunderstand the feelings of right or wrong; you'll just know. Returning to Rocky's life as the example of this, the more he puts Braveheart in charge, the more he naturally declutters his mind, and the more he'll naturally enable the disassembling of his old life and the assembling of his new one. The more Rocky knows what he wants, is acting on what he wants, and isn't participating in anything that doesn't connect him to his deepest desires, the more connected he will feel to his purpose and presence from moment to moment.

The same goes for you.

It takes patience and commitment to integrate the various parts of yourself. Although committing to—and following through with—being authentic doesn't mean all your problems are going to be solved tomorrow, it does mean that you're not holding yourself back from what you need that's going to serve you.

As you become more authentic, you may go through an uncomfortable adjustment, because when one part of your social or familial ecosystem shifts, the rest will too. But know that this too will pass. When you change the steps to the dance and live as the authentic expression of yourself, you're bound to stir things up for those around you. The tide of your evolution raises all boats in your harbor, so stay the course and honor yourself, no matter how uncomfortable it might seem in the moment.

Authenticity takes practice, but over time what you create will be magical.

You've begun to strip away the most deep-set obstacles on your journey and you are now able to dismantle your old belief systems, peeling them away, one at a time. This is required in order to be who you really are. You are dismantling the layers of shame, unworthiness, poverty consciousness, or any other belief that does not connect you to the life you desire. You're assembling your new life with the layers of how capable, radiant, strong, and brave you are, and you are able to live out more of your favorite qualities from your 100 Things list.

Not only did Dorothy see that all the power was within her, but her seeing her truth allowed others on the journey to do so also. Dorothy saw her power and so did the Tin Man, the Scarecrow, and the Cowardly Lion. As it was for Dorothy and Braveheart, the greatness within you has access to the infinite power of the universe when you recognize who you're not, realize who you are, and reveal the many layers of yourself to the world.

EXERCISE: UNPACKING THE 4 Ds

Sit in a quiet place, when you can be uninterrupted, and daydream about what your life might look like in five years if you were to create and get everything you ever wanted. It's a big question, I know. You can use your character archetype as a way to ease into the visioning process.

Next let's unpack your vision through the 4 Ds:

1. **Desire**—What do you really want?

2. **Design**—You can be anything. Are you smart, sexy, fit, a great parent, successful, a leader, a teacher, a healer?

3. **Decide**—Decide, with intensity, what you will *never* have in your life again.

4. **Detach**—How can you change yourself and your behaviors, detaching yourself from previous patterns, so that your actions are in alignment with your desires?

Consider how your answers shape who you authentically are. On a blank page in your journal, spend time brainstorming what your best self would think, do, or say as a response to each of the 4 Ds. Think *big*.

How would the version of you in five years from now fill in the answers to the 4 Ds? I want you to stretch your imagination, and remember, you're creating as you write.

In the next chapter, we will lay the groundwork for creating new beliefs by establishing affirmations and learning ways to change our thoughts and words.

CHAPTER 8

THE HEART OF IT ALL

"The limits of my language are the limits of my world."

—LUDWIG WITTGENSTEIN

We have talked so much about changing our life from the inside out, beginning with our brain, our story, and our chemistry. We established our very own Do Not Say lists, and now we dive into the most exciting territory: creating our life with the power of our words.

AWAKENING TO MY CONSCIOUSNESS

From the time I was a little girl, I knew there was a certain magic in most ancient traditions and philosophies, even though I didn't know exactly what it was. Whenever PBS aired a special on science, the earth, or ancient history, I sat glued to the television. I was like a sponge, absorbing everything I could about the Sumerians, Egyptians, Mayans and Incas, plate tectonics, the cycles and eras of the earth, cultural superstitions, mythology, sinkholes, and black holes. Simply put, learning about the mysteries of the universe was my saving grace in a childhood of uncertainty. I lost entire afternoons looking for four-leaf clovers in the grass in my aunt and uncle's backyard so I could make a wish. Even back then

I believed that I could change my reality . . . if I could only find one of those tiny green talismans.

It wasn't long before my fascinations became obsessions. Between all my preoccupations—science, cosmology, and archeology—I sensed an invisible connective thread. It was a relief to learn that one of my favorite scientists, Albert Einstein, was as equally committed to understanding God as he was to understanding the universe. Throughout my teens and into my 20s, I continued studying philosophy, world religions, ethics, and ancient history—and science, of course. When my daughter was born with severe brain damage in 1992, and when my son Keagan was diagnosed with autism a few years later, all that time learning about the brain and about the human spirit paved my way toward a better understanding of what was going on. I saw it all, from the yoga sutras to Stephen Hawking, as a bunch of different ways to talk about the same thing: the experience of being human is intimately connected to awakening our consciousness.

THE DOWNWARD DOG OF SELF-REALIZATION

In a matter of months, my divorce went from manageably stressful to downright vicious and nasty. And naturally, when the divorce proceedings went south, I went with it. My nervous system was so shot from all the destructive interactions with my soon-to-be-ex-husband that it wasn't long before I could barely get out of bed in the morning. On days when I did go to work, I hid under my desk in my office, crying half the day, and having my assistant filter all interactions, calls, or requests for my time the other half of the day. I had gone from feeling like Superwoman to wondering how long it would be until my business imploded or I collapsed beneath the weight of stress. I was miserable, and I had gotten so used to hearing my own complaints that I didn't notice how negative I had become. It became my norm, and, in rare moments of clarity, I hardly recognized myself anymore.

Through determination and a healthy dose of synchronicity, I eventually found myself at a Louise Hay retreat in Tucson, Arizona, at Miraval Resort. I desperately wanted to get some intense work-outs in while there, but the only exercise classes offered were yoga. It was at Miraval's yoga studio, with world-renowned instructors, in a beautiful and inviting studio that featured grand, sweeping views of Arizona's peaceful mountains, that I got a taste of yoga beyond the fitness yoga I'd only done at the gym.

In that first class at Miraval, my internal mind chatter was so loud and berating that I thought I might be speaking it instead of just thinking it. I looked around, but no one else seemed to hear it, and it certainly seemed like I was the only one trying to quiet the incessant loop of self-talk. I didn't love the yoga practice, but I didn't hate it like I thought I would either; and when I was done with a class, I always felt a little better than when I walked in. I can't say exactly why, but after that experience in Arizona at Miraval, I got a taste for yoga. Once home I eased my way into the yoga classes back at the gym, each time feeling relief—albeit temporary—from the noise inside my mind.

After Miraval I would take a journal to class with me filled with my own mantras, from simple affirmations I wanted to embody, like *I am love* or *I embrace kindness*, to the ancient Hawaiian *ho'oponopono* mantra of *I'm sorry; please forgive me; thank you; I love you.* Eventually something clicked. All the understanding I once had about creating my own reality snapped back into focus, and I knew that I could find my relief and myself again, whether I was on—or off—the yoga mat.

THE HEART OF CONSCIOUS COMMUNICATIONS

As I've told you, I developed Conscious Communications for my collections business, and at first I thought that was all it was going to be good for. This was great, because let me tell you, it was *definitely* good for business. I have so many stories of turning around seemingly impossible calls with irate clients and defensive debtors—and all it takes is just a few simple words. One of my employees, Misty, was contacted by a client who was frustrated that we had not collected on his account and demanded to know why. She validated the client by letting him know that she understood his frustration and that she was happy to set proper expectations on the recovery of his account. By validating, planting a seed of happiness, and setting proper expectations, she was able to defuse the client to the point that he was laughing by the end of the call. It's as simple as that!

And it works among those of us in the office as well. John manages an IT team, and he has found that using Conscious Communications allows him to maintain excellent morale within that team, even when they're faced with tasks that seem overwhelming. For example, by ending a request with "The great news is that after we're done with this, our other responsibilities will be easier to complete," he can basically eliminate the chance of someone complaining about that task, keeping everyone motivated and even excited to get to work.

But it wasn't until I started hearing my employees talk about the power of this system in their *personal lives* that it really hit me how powerful it can be. Misty—the same Misty who calmed the frustrated client—has a five-year-old daughter who is learning Conscious Communications. She uses it daily without even realizing what she's doing! Misty started using it when her daughter began demanding candy all the time. Instead of saying no, Misty would tell her, "I'm happy to give you an apple." It took a few months of consistent practice, but eventually Misty's daughter stopped asking for candy all the time. And best of all, Misty's daughter has learned to use Conscious Communications too.

So how can you use words to benefit *you?* Well, take a page from Misty's book and knock off that negative talk, for starters. But then take it a step further and use powerfully positive words. We know that the words we say have a big impact on us, and science can now affirm what the ancient traditions have known for millennia. For example, the breakdown of the popularized ancient eastern word *abracadabra* is "I will create as I speak." When I learned this, I was floored with confirmation. And just like in John 1:1, the Bible says, "In the beginning was the Word, and the Word was with God, and the Word was God," the connection between speech and creation is clear and powerful. Our words are an act of creation, just as we too are individual acts of creation. From the mantras of Buddhists to the prayers of Jewish, Christian, and Muslim devotees to Native American tribal chants and rain dances, the creation and repetition of words or phrases becomes an instrument of thought—a tool to help reprogram our mind, and our life experiences.

As I linked up certain concepts like *abracadabra,* mantras, and prayer, I began to see that the connection to consciousness and creating your own reality wasn't just about a bottom line–driven business strategy. It was about a deliberately crafted life experience, first and foremost.

SELF=TALK CREATES YOUR BLUEPRINT FOR LIFE

Before the idea for this book came to me, I remember telling everybody that one day I was going to write a book. That was my clear ambition, but the only problem was that I always followed it up with "but I'm not a writer." It seems strange to say a desire in one half of a sentence and then follow it up with a barrier belief in the same breath, but this is much more common than you might think.

I realized I was sabotaging my desire to publish a book long before I could even begin the process. From the time this was pointed out to me—that I wanted to publish a book but always followed this statement up with "but I'm not a writer"—it took me almost two more years to change that as my mantra.

When I was in the limbo of knowing I had a barrier belief attached at the hip of my desire but wanting to let that limiting belief go, I had to focus on going easy on myself. I reminded myself that since we have 60,000 thoughts in a day, and 95 percent are the same as yesterday, any mantra I had that reinforced negative beliefs had been there for a *long* time. In all likelihood I had probably repeated it in my head at least a million times. It was in my best interest to be patient with myself as I reprogrammed my beliefs.

173

If you're still wondering why (and how) self-talk creates reality, let's start with this: The words you repeat and replay to and about yourself, whether internally or externally, become a powerful guiding force in how you make choices. We learned earlier that every choice you make will literally change the probable outcomes of your life. Your words—your mantras—are part of your daily practice, even if you don't realize it. As it is with any daily practice, the more you choose and rechoose a word, phrase, or topic to focus on, the more automatic the practice becomes. You know that daily practices, over time, can change you. So if you want the outcome of you, your personality, and your perception of the world to land on the favorable side, it's important to stay with your daily practice of choosing your words, and your life blueprint, carefully.

CHANGE YOUR THOUGHTS AND YOUR WORDS

Our mind creates our speech, and through those words our ideas come alive. You may have seen the phrase *change your thoughts, change your life*, and maybe you heard about it through the late Wayne Dyer's book by the same title. This notion of changing your thoughts is ancient, as it comes from the Tao Te Ching, which is made up of 81 verses dictated by Chinese philosopher Lao Tzu about the nature of human existence. I absolutely agree with the idea that you can change your life by changing your thoughts . . . but have you ever tried changing your thoughts at the source in the mind? I have, and it feels nearly impossible.

As we've talked about in earlier chapters, your thoughts are only one part of the feedback loop. Since your words reflect the content of your mind, if you can capture and change the words, in time they will change their reflection in your head. Whether it's empowering or disempowering, what you say instructs your reticular activating system (RAS) to search for confirmation.

If I talk about what I want, I'm training my brain to find those things. When I talk about what I don't want or complain about what's happening, I'm *also* training my brain to find *those* things. Let's return to the earlier example of how, for most of my adult life, I said that I wanted to write a book. Then I started getting more specific with that mantra: *I want Louise Hay to publish my book.* When I got comfortable *saying* that I would publish a book, I realized I wanted *Louise Hay* to publish my book. That's a pretty big desire, and yet I still didn't actually believe I could write a book.

Nevertheless, the mantra made me actually notice when people asked me to write a book about Conscious Communications, or finance, or even increasing conscious awareness, whereas before I hadn't seen or heard those requests at all. I also started seeing synchronicities around writing that continued opening the path, one step at a time, to this reality. Because I started saying these affirmations, that I would write a book, and that I would have it published by Louise Hay, I was open to the ideas that came.

Each time you make a statement like, *I don't have enough money, I can't afford that, I'm going to have to file bankruptcy,* or *I'm always broke,* you are reinforcing the pathway that created that situation in the first place. Your RAS will continue to seek out experiences to support having a poverty consciousness.

Instead, immerse yourself in the life you want to create through deliberately aligned speech. This doesn't mean lying or deceiving yourself; you're simply reframing your perception of reality. Consider the words you say to be direct instructions to your inner core consciousness, or subconscious. Your words condition your subconscious, and if you are intentional and determined about it, you can effectively use the words you speak to bypass any current, unwanted, or outdated programming to create new neural pathways and new beliefs about life.

LAYING IT ALL ON THE (MASSAGE) TABLE

I'm a single mom, and my kids see their dad two weekends each month, which means that any alone time I get is treasured. About a week before I began writing this chapter, I made an appointment with my friend and licensed massage therapist, Jessica, for one of my personal self-care days. I've gone to Jessica for massages for at least five years, and not only is she an incredible healer with her hands, but she also has a degree in psychology and she's a Reiki master. And best of all, she believes in talking about things during massage as a way to release them from your body, knowing that things get stuck in your body, your muscles, and your cells.

Prior to the appointment, I came across an audio recording of author and speaker Neville Goddard's speech entitled "Self-Talk Creates Reality," and its message lined up so perfectly with Conscious Communications that I listened to the audio on repeat. I was particularly motivated by some difficult exchanges I'd recently had with my ex-husband, and I was using the Neville Goddard audio to help me reprogram my negative thoughts about my ex.

I decided that while I was lying on the massage table, I would focus on my Magic 8, which is a list of eight goals and desires that, when they come to pass, will feel magical. I figured I'd use the time on the massage table to give birth to the ideas for this chapter, and because my Magic 8 list is, in essence, an affirmations list, it seemed like a done deal.

That is, until I was facedown on the massage table and started to try. I began my attempt to focus on self-talk with regard to my ex-husband, the very first affirmation on my Magic 8 list, which is: *I have a peaceful relationship with my ex-husband. We are raising our children in a mutually beneficial way, and we instill morals and values in them that support their growth into happy and healthy adults.*

It didn't work. I struggled and struggled to recite these affirmations about my relationship with my ex for 40 minutes, but I simply couldn't. I lay there, tense, with my mind and body totally disconnected, and I couldn't enjoy the massage, nor could I experience even an ounce of relief from the negative feedback loop inside my head. I felt like I was going crazy.

Instead of the truths I walked in hoping to repeat to myself, all I could see, feel, and hear were thoughts of doom and gloom. Here are a few of my thoughts from that day:

How am I going to have a peaceful relationship with him when he hangs up on me all the time?

Not only does my ex contribute very little financially, but now Keagan has an F in Spanish and a D in English, and he hasn't done two weeks' worth of homework! How can we have a peaceful relationship when he refuses to cooperate with me in disciplining our son?

The moment I tried to get into a fantasy where everything was peaceful and glorious, *this* was the poison floating around in my mind.

I couldn't stand the tortured silence of lying there with my negative thoughts, so I spoke up and said something to Jessica. I wanted to present my intention, my affirmations, and my frustrations calmly, but all I could say about what I was feeling, and about Neville Goddard's talk was this:

"It should be so easy. I don't understand why I am having such a hard time controlling my thoughts."

Jessica continued the massage and gently replied by asking me questions to help me work through my frustrations. Each question irritated me even more than the last. I felt my shoulders tensing up, felt the temperature rising in the room, and with each answer, the lump grew bigger in my throat. I didn't want to answer another question. I felt massive resistance and a strong desire to pop up off the table and leave, which has never happened to me before. But I didn't leave. Not only do I trust Jessica, but I also trusted her process, even though I wanted to run away. I just leaned into the pain and sadness.

I had to be honest about things I was very uncomfortable admitting, like how attached I was to the feelings I have about my ex, mostly because they are easily justified. But at this point, I didn't want to feel justified; I wanted to have peace. Most of my answers to Jessica's questions were about my resentment about being mistreated by him and about his lack of support both financially and as a co-parent. My tears streamed through the face space in the massage table, and I tried to breathe deeply as I cried.

We talked more about words and thoughts and the importance of the feelings underneath the words we say—our affirmations. All I really wanted was a peaceful relationship with my ex-husband, but I couldn't get past my fears and resentments. Even the act of focusing on my desired outcome triggered more fear and resentment.

"It's a good thing you can be grateful that you don't need his financial support," Jessica noted.

I squirmed. "I don't feel like that right now because of that giant, unexpected bill."

Now it wasn't just sadness, frustration, or resistance brewing in me; I also felt anger and powerlessness toward the situation. This wasn't just about my ex now; it included the general feeling of being overwhelmed, and that I couldn't keep balancing the weight of the world on my shoulders anymore.

"You're such a powerful woman. I know you have an incredible ability to conquer these obstacles," Jessica said.

I sobbed, trying to allow her hands to move the tension out of my upper back. "The thing is, I just don't want to anymore."

It was quiet for a moment, and then she said, "You have been taking care of everything on your own for so long—even since childhood—without support. And you've hit your limit with carrying everyone's load. It's overwhelming that you are doing it on your own. It seems like at your core, what you really want is unconditional love and support."

With that, it was as if the faucet of tears turned off right when my light bulb came on. The essence of what I really wanted—and was asking the universe to provide me with—was unconditional love and support. And I didn't have to get it from my ex in order to have it. This truth felt so aligned because it didn't create more internal conflict or trigger resentment for me.

What I learned from that experience is that there is a simple process to discovering what it is you really want or believe you can have or experience. If you're experiencing any resistance or uncertainty about what you want, you must start by unraveling the knot.

Start with your desire, and if you're not sure that it's the "right" desire, that's okay. Just try it on, like you would try on a shirt when you're shopping for a new outfit.

Next ask yourself, *What kind of person could have this desire or experience? What qualities would that person have? Are those qualities in line with who I want to be?*

For me, in order to receive unconditional love and support, I would need to be vulnerable and willing to ask for—and receive—others' help.

Then look closely at what is in the way between where your life currently is and where you want to go. Start with the bigger things, and break each of those items into smaller bits until you can see the pieces that are holding you back.

Understanding that every time you take a step in a new direction you change your future probabilities, ask yourself, *What can I do differently today that will adjust my life in a different direction?* It's all part of the process of creating the life you want through identifying your true desires.

I'll often hear from friends that they can't say any affirmations because nothing they affirm feels true. Whenever I hear this, I encourage them to keep going, because I know that getting clarity comes when you're trying to affirm something that's *not* your truth. It's like trying on outfit after outfit after outfit, and finally realizing what you need or want to wear in order to feel your best. It's truly a trial-and-error process.

As *A Course in Miracles* says, this process is an act of creating miracles, since a miracle is but a shift in perception. You create these miracles, both big and small, through your self-talk and through your deliberate affirmations. I shifted my perception that day from wanting my ex-husband to step up and support his kids to understanding that what I really wanted was unconditional love and support in my life. By the end of the day, I was in tears again, but this time it was because I could see all the unconditional love and support from everyone around me. As in

Dorothy's story, everyone and everything I loved had been there all along. I knew I had experienced a miracle.

TYPES OF AFFIRMATIONS

There are as many unique ways to affirm things in the world as there are possible thoughts in a person, but from my research and experience, I have found there to be five general types of affirmations:

1. **Negative and disempowering affirmations.** These express criticism of yourself or others, like *I am so stupid* or *I hate that she always* . . . They also include weak speech, with words like *try* and *should*—saying "I should call my mom" is very different from actually calling your mom.

2. **Releasing statements.** These are powerful statements of what you will no longer accept as your truth. This is an affirmation that is in line with making a Decision with a big *D*, one that is charged with deep emotion and intention. For example: *I release my fear of abandonment.*

3. ***I am* statements.** These affirmations declare the qualities, personality traits, lifestyle choices, and values you want to embody in your life. By stating these desires using the opening phrase *I am*, you trigger your reticular activating system to scan your experiences for evidence to support this new way of being.

4. **Asking statements.** These affirmations involve asking the universe to bring or guide you to encounters or experiences that will move you toward your desires, like:

   Guide me . . .
   Help me . . .

Show me . . .
Bring me toward the thoughts and choices that
support my goals.

5. **Gratitude statements.** We've talked about the
    positive impact of gratitude on our life and our
    focus. This kind of affirmation—being grateful for
    what you have, for what works and feels good in
    your life—signals your RAS to continue identifying
    those people, feelings, or experiences that trigger the
    feeling of gratitude.

For more examples of different kinds of affirmations, check
out my website, MaryShores.com. You'll find hundreds of them
there, as well as some inspiration to help you create yours too.

Some people choose to repeat their affirmations out loud.
Others decide to write them down. I've found it to be particularly
helpful to write out one page of affirmations every morning. It
puts me in a great frame of mind to start my day, while helping
to create new neural pathways.

I suggest framing affirmations as if they've already come to
pass. While this is something I often recommend, this needs to be
handled carefully. If you're between jobs and you want to attract a
great job, you can't say, *I have an amazing job that makes me fulfilled
both financially and spiritually*—because that isn't true yet, and the
affirmation will ignite more resistance than before you even began
the exercise. On the flip side, though, you can say affirmations
such as, *Guide me to opportunities that fulfill me, both financially and
spiritually*, or *Help me be in the right place at the right time.*

The magic here is that the grip you have on your resistance
will eventually loosen, but only if you commit to the practice
with repetition. I'm not advocating affirmations that you're not
comfortable with. On the contrary. If all you can do is declare
what you're no longer willing to welcome in your life, start there.

As you deliberately choose one or two affirmations each day,
a good framework is to flow between releasing, asking, *I am* statements, and gratitude—something like, *I release my fear of abandonment*, then *I am worthy and deserving of unconditional love and support.*

If you're really stuck, move on to something else. Be willing to be a little curious, and look for things you're grateful for in other areas of life. It can be as simple as: *I am grateful for my full head of hair.*

The point of all this is to move you up the frequency scale of emotions. When you can be grateful for even the softness of the pillow under your head, it helps your emotions move up, which broadens your perspective and allows you to see things you hadn't seen before.

COMMIT TO CREATING NEW BELIEFS

Just as gratitude, focus, and cleanse or clog are ways to instill new beliefs, creating, adopting, and using affirmations are other ways to expedite this process. You're going to affect the whole circle and change your neural pathways no matter which part of the feedback loop you interrupt.

Using affirmations primes your brain to make choices to help you create that reality. Your RAS knows what you want and links up to a higher power, however you define it, to inspire you to take action and connect you to your dream.

Here are a few ways you can play with creating affirmations that are true for you today, but that also offer an opportunity for you to grow:

- Write affirmations that begin with things like *Guide me to* or *Bring me toward* and think of an experience or person that could get you closer to your goal.

- Collect the compliments you receive and turn them into affirmations.

- Decide what you want and make it into an affirmation, such as *I want to experience . . .*

By making your affirmations real and personal, you will make different choices. Affirmations program your brain, creating new neural pathways, causing you to look for things or bringing you ideas that will make those affirmations true. Little by little, and sometimes in quantum leaps, you're getting closer to what it is you truly want to experience.

Remember that for years and years, your inner monologue, personal mantra, or patterns and beliefs have circulated throughout your brain and created neural networks that make those patterns the natural default. In order for a new affirmation to take root—and really begin working—it's important that you commit to the habit of saying your affirmations every day.

The person you are today is learned and conditioned over years and years. Just like an athlete needs to train, you must condition your speech if you want to have certain experiences. You become what you think about most of the time, and everything about your personality, your behaviors, your thoughts, and your words comes from deep programming.

If you want your affirmations to create new neural pathways, that happens through repetition, just like building a muscle. Creating and committing to the practice of using your new affirmations will help you be more authentically you, the self that you truly desire to be—100 percent uniquely you.

As your affirmations start to take shape and embed themselves in your regular speech, you'll find yourself starting to feel better, which will help you create more opportunities for yourself. I'll say it again: repetition is the only way affirmations get programmed inside of you. The ease with which you can recall your childhood phone number is proof of this. The more you commit to a new way of speaking that aligns with your desired behavior or outcome, the more quickly you're going to manifest that.

100 THINGS I LOVE ABOUT ME

A few years ago on National Women's Day, I was invited to be a guest on a local radio show. From what the interviewer said, it seemed there were hundreds of women who were eager and excited at the prospect of creating their own 100 Things lists. Remember doing that back in Chapter 2? That list has gotten me through some of my hardest moments—particularly since it is, at heart, a list of real and true affirmations.

It seemed that everywhere I went in the weeks that followed that interview, people were doing the 100 Things list exercise. Some of them, my barista included, even randomly came up to me to share their "Oh my God!" moments. I experienced a kindred energy with all these women because I had shared my numbers 99 and 100, and my subsequent light-bulb moment, on the radio show.

For my numbers 99 and 100, I had written down *I am radiant* and *I am a magnetic, powerful creator.* I wouldn't have been able to see those truths about myself if I hadn't peeled back the other 98 layers in my list of 100 things I loved about myself. Because of the list, I could start seeing these things in me.

After I had completed my list, people were constantly complimenting me, and it was a compliment that I hadn't received before. It was:

You're so radiant!

Now, that's a very particular compliment. It flooded in within a two-week period after I had finished my list, and for good reason. To begin with, because I uncovered that truth about myself, it was no longer buried. I walked around smiling, cheerful, and glowing. People complimented my radiance because I *was* radiant. Second, I'm of the belief that the thoughts, the gratitude, the energy, and the intention floated out into the collective consciousness—I was radiant, and others *could see* my radiance. The energy of your intentions impacts and affects your energy field.

Whether it's in the 100 Things list, the gratitude text, your daily affirmations—either writing them out or saying them in the mirror—it doesn't matter. The synchronicity is that when I wrote something specific on my 100 Things list, it started showing up for me. It did for the women listening to the radio program that day, and it will for you too.

MANAGING THE RESISTANCE

If you're working on creating your affirmations but you're feeling stuck because nothing seems true or right to you, stay with it and explore. There are solutions there. In the same way you would explore getting clarity around what your desires are in the first place, there's also a process for moving out of resistance to creating a certain affirmation and toward affirming something that feels great.

Here are some steps to help you manage the resistance:

1. **Name the resistance.** What are you feeling? What do you want?

2. **Identify why you are justifying not having what you want.** Then go deeper: why don't you *really* have what you want?

3. **Explore the goal.** Who is the kind of person who would have the thing or experience you want?

4. **Research your role models.** Identify the qualities that person would have *in order to have the experience/ thing* that you want.

5. **Get honest with yourself.** What actions are you taking—or are you willing to take—to develop the qualities that will open up the probabilities of fulfilling your desire?

6. **Start affirming.** Using a variety of the types of affirmations we've discussed—asking, gratitude, *I am* statements, and so on—affirm that you embody the qualities you need to create the new desires.

When you're done with the process above, it'll be important to circle back to address the fears woven into the "why you don't have it" question. By now you'll have begun to dismantle the limiting beliefs around this fear, so this next step will be easier at this stage than if you were to do it earlier: Create an affirmation that is the *opposite* of the fear. Instead of *I'm afraid I would have*

to compromise my values to get . . . , flip it to be something like *I embrace my value, and this trait is what attracts the experience/person/goal.* You're a work in progress—as you always will be—and so are your affirmations. Revisit and repeat these processes as often as necessary if you find yourself hitting a speed bump of resistance and needing a little push over to the other side.

BECOMING A WRITER

As you read earlier in this chapter, my desire for Hay House to publish my book was an affirmation I had linked with a mantra that I wasn't a writer. Because of my business-minded, solution-focused orientation, when the desire to write and publish a book got big enough for me to take action, despite my limiting beliefs, I began approaching the desire a little differently than before.

Instead of affirming that *I'm not a writer,* I reframed it to be: *How can I become a writer?*

This small pivot opened my awareness so that I attended a Hay House Writer's Workshop where the keynote speaker was *Notes from the Universe* creator, Mike Dooley.

From the stage Mike educated the audience about some of the various ways we could take our message and turn it into a book. I listened eagerly, trying to find my *how.* In the exact moment that Mike told us to record our workshop, have it transcribed, and work with an editor to massage it into a book, in a rapid-fire unfolding in my mind's eye, I saw the blueprint laid out before me of all the points and plans I needed to—and absolutely could—take to reach my goal. The clarity and the knowing was like a bolt of lightning. I was so full of excitement from everything I had learned that day that the three-hour drive home from Chicago felt like a 20-minute drive. I could literally feel myself climbing the frequency scale.

In the blink of an eye, my belief system adjusted that day. Instead of *but I'm not a writer,* I now felt like a writer. Furthermore, I became 100 percent confident that I have a story to tell and lessons to teach.

This is the power of the question, *How can I?* The *I'm not a writer* mantra changed the instant I saw *how I could be* a writer, and it reprogrammed all my old patterns and beliefs. I share this to say that although repetition of an affirmation is important for you to create a new belief and experience the manifestation around the new belief, not all neural pathways are programmed in the same way. Moments when your mind is blown also make for swift and easy reprogramming and creation of new neural pathways.

EXERCISE: THREE STEPS TO CREATE ROCKING SELF-TALK

As you can see, the process of using deliberate affirmations is incredibly powerful. If you've been taking action throughout this chapter, you'll already recognize the changes in your life. But in the event that you need some clearer direction, here is a simple three-step process to help you create your rocking affirmations.

Open a blank page in your journal, and label it "Affirmations."

1. **State it.** Make a quick bulleted list of five things about yourself that you are fed up with or are sick and tired of. Then, next to each behavior, write out something that fuels your desire and emotional conviction. Underline the place in the sentence where the feelings run high, and flip it into an *I will never* or *Never again will I* statement.

    For example, if you want to quit smoking cigarettes, and a teacher remarked that your kid smells like she's been smoking, use this as the emotional fuel to make your big-*D* Decision and declare your desire to stop smoking, which could be: *I will never smoke again!*

    This is the beginning of you creating powerful affirmations that will change your neural pathways and change your life.

2. **Repeat it.** Refer back to the list of 100 things you love about yourself. Copy five of the statements onto your affirmations page in your journal. Keep them simple and accessible so that you don't freeze in the face of resistance. Try statements like: *I am loving* or *I am radiant.*

3. **Dream it.** Ask yourself, *What would my life look like if everything was exactly as I want it to be?* If you could have or experience anything you desire, without limitation, what would that look like? In this step, spend a few minutes dreaming up ways your life can and will look when you feel the way you want to feel. Frame it in the present tense, as though it is your current reality. For example, a simple place to start that I've found many people resonate with is: *My life is full of laughter, friendship, and love.*

Start repeating your *I will never again,* your *I am,* and your *My life is* statements as part of your daily routine of self-care. Say and write out these statements as if the experiences and feelings have already arrived. You don't have to add this into your day flawlessly in order to see improvements in your life, but the more regularly you either say or write out these affirmations, the more your life will change.

It takes work to become the person who embodies what you want. It's important that you're focused on being that person instead of just having an arbitrary goal, because if the goal doesn't line up with the person you want to be, you won't create the necessary circumstances to have that experience. Affirm the qualities you want to have in order for you to create lasting change.

You're probably able to see a shift in your life already by doing the work so far in this book. To expedite change, here are some things to always keep in mind:

- **Be aware when something is not your truth.** Look at it as a fact-finding mission, and be grateful you saw something that didn't work for you. It means you're that much closer to seeing and experiencing what *does* work.

- **Remove behaviors that do not connect you to what you want.** If you constantly find yourself participating in activities, reactions, or behaviors that are in conflict with your desired outcome, be willing to let those go and replace them with choices that are more in line with your dreams.

- **Create your beliefs.** Believe that every step you take in a new direction opens up thousands of new possibilities.

There's magic in the interplay of your gratitude list, your gratitude club, and your affirmations. The more daily practices you do, the faster you accelerate and magnify your manifesting synchronicities. It's too perfect to be random.

In the next chapter, we'll bring all the pieces of information you've learned together with your new tools. There is only one piece left to complete the puzzle of creating your dream life: taking action.

CHAPTER 9

THE LAST PIECE OF THE PUZZLE: TAKING ACTION WITH THE END IN MIND

"Think like a queen. A queen is not afraid to fail. Failure is another stepping stone to greatness."

— OPRAH WINFREY

You've made it this far. Now what? It's time to start utilizing all the tools you have gained along this journey. It's time to welcome your new life.

CONSCIOUSLY CREATING YOUR MENU

Anything and everything you could ever want is on the menu of your life, and from it you get to choose your experiences.

If you really believed that you could have, do, or be anything you wanted, how would your life change? Could you really live your dream life? Well, I have great news: you can. You just have to put your dreams on the menu.

When you step back and look at life objectively, you can see that when a person's life changes, it happens in one of two ways:

1. **Gradual, incremental changes**. These are caused
    by the small improvements we make every day. Over
    time they add up to a transformation, all beginning
    with one step in a different direction.

2. **Major choices, or decision points.** These are the
    pivot points that determine the path our life takes,
    and with each new pivot we face a new direction
    and a whole new set of probabilities. Each choice
    can open up an entirely new destiny.

Think about the last time you went out to eat. The host or
hostess handed you a menu. By definition the options were limited, based on the type of restaurant you were at or by the kinds of
food the chef liked to cook. The restaurant decided exactly what
to put on the menu, and those were your choices. Now imagine
just the opposite. Imagine that you could decide what was on that
menu! Anything you could possibly desire would be made for you.

That'd be pretty great, right? Try applying this idea to your
life. If your life is your menu, and only you get to decide what's
on it, think about what that opens up for you! But it works the
other way too—if you don't put what you really want on your
menu, there's no way you're going to get it.

The thing is, you can only have things on your menu that *you*
believe you deserve. Every choice you make in your life is determined by evaluating the options *you* decide are available to you.
So I'm going to ask you one seriously important question: what
do you want on *your* menu?

Right now everything you experience in your life is there
because at one point it was on your menu and you chose it. What
you're looking forward to, what you're worried about, even the
design of your life—the menu itself—and each of your choices
in life are there because of your decision to have those choices to
begin with. That list of worries and fears that you have are actually on your menu—and you put them there.

Once you've filled your menu with choices you actually want,
the next step is to believe those options are really available to
you. And they are—you are the only one who can say they aren't.

Want to travel the world? Put it on your menu! There *is* a way to make that happen. Want to start a nonprofit organization to help stray animals? Put it on your menu! I promise, there is a way to make that happen. Any dream, any job, any life, any option you desire, put it on your menu!

And there's one more thing I want you to put on there. You know how when you go to a fancy restaurant there's that dish that doesn't even have a price listed? The one that just says *market price* or *MP*, and you can feel your wallet shrinking even as you read the description? That "market price" item, that one dream that maybe you don't *quite* believe is possible—make sure you put that on your menu, because that's the most important one of all. That is your Greatness Potential.

If your Greatness Potential menu item doesn't immediately come to mind, think about this: what are you best at in life? Remember the list of 100 things we made back in Chapter 2? Take a look at that. In fact, take a look at all the exercises we've done together—they will tell you your Greatness Potential.

I know that my Greatness Potential is to make a huge difference in the collections industry. I will have an impact—I *do* have an impact. I am making the world a better place. But I didn't always know that! I've gone from breakdown to breakthrough as I teetered on the verge of bankruptcy, lost $180,000 in the year after my divorce, and struggled to raise my special needs child without support—I am an example of someone whose life shattered. But after a lot of work, I realized my ultimate potential. I understand people. I understand psychology. And I asked myself, *What difference can I make in the world with this gift?*

That is Greatness Potential.

If you look at your list of 100 things and you see that you are an incredible teacher, what can you do to serve the world as a teacher? If you're an artist, how will your art improve the world?

At the core of this process of remaking your life, you're learning to trust your intuition. As you get closer to that place where you can trust yourself, you become more willing to get rid of the layers of fear and barrier beliefs that hold you back from the life you want. If you're driven by fear, your intuition is guiding you based on barrier beliefs, and you're going to make some awkward or incorrect choices from that place. By discarding those barrier beliefs that were rooted in old, outdated situations, you create space to grow into new possibilities. Ultimately your focus, programming, chemistry, and intuition are all at play here, and none is more important than the other. They make up the way you see the world—they help you create your menu.

EXERCISE: PUT IT ON THE MEN

I've broken your menu into seven categories—health, finances, career, personal relationships, self-care, spirituality, and your Greatness Potential. I want you to list at least five things you want on your menu in the first six categories, and *definitely* fill in that "market price" item!

Once you've filled it out, I want you to believe that they really are available to you. *You* get to decide. Then write down just one step, big or small, that you could take to make each of these things happen. Lastly, take action!

Health _____

_____

_____

_____

Finances _____

_____

_____

_____

Career _____

_____

_____

_____

Personal Relationships _____

_____

_____

_____

Self-Care _____

_____

_____

_____

Spirituality _____

_____

_____

_____

Greatness Potential _____

_____

_____

_____

BEGIN WITH THE END IN MIND

That exercise asked you to take action . . . but I know sometimes that's the hardest part. These dreams, these goals, they can seem so impossible that we don't even know where to start. In July 2015 I spoke at Lily Dale Assembly about my one-page action plan, a plan I have used to accomplish everything I've achieved in my adult life, big or small. At Lily Dale, one of the attendees, let's call her Maura, had a dream. She wanted to create a healing center, and she had such a powerful vision for it. She had in mind a gorgeous domed facility with pools of essential oils and healing herbs. The pathways would be made of smooth stones that hit acupuncture points in the feet as they were walked on. It was incredible—basically Disneyland for adults.

But she had no idea how to turn it from a dream into a reality. It was too overwhelming. So we broke it down—what were six things that Maura needed in order to open her healing center?

1. **Cash.** Something as beautiful as that requires a lot of money!

2. **Business coaching.** Maura didn't have a lot of business savvy, and with something this expensive, you need to know what you're doing.

3. **Location.** Where is this healing center going to be? It needs to be remote enough to be peaceful, but still accessible.

4. **Partners/Employees.** Obviously Maura wouldn't be able to do all this herself.

5. **Legal advice.** There are all kinds of potential pitfalls in opening a new business. What sorts of permits are required by the government? What sorts of codes need to be met for the accommodations? And how much space for how many people would the healing center require?

6. **Advertising.** Maura needed to get people excited about visiting!

Taken as a whole, this list still seems pretty overwhelming. There's a lot to get done. But then you break it down into *how* to get what you need. Let's take point 1, cash. Maura wrote down three action items that she could do in order to get the financing for her healing center in place:

- Investigate how to find investors.

- Talk to a bank manager about getting a business loan.

- Find extra revenue (pick up an extra shift at work, do freelance work on the side, make things to sell on Etsy, et cetera).

We did that for each and every one of her points, until she knew exactly what she needed to do. That didn't mean it was going to be easy! But in order to make your dream a reality, you have to take action. Putting your dream on the menu is the first and most important step. But taking action is how you achieve your dreams.

EXERCISE: YOUR ONE-PAGE ACTION PLAN

In the space below, write out your number-one biggest vision—your "dream vision"—for what you want to make happen. Focus on only one, though I'm sure you have plenty more. Take a few moments to write out what it would look like when your vision came to pass.

What is your vision?

My dream vision is:

Example: My dream vision is to open a flower shop.

Then, in each of the spaces given, write out specific things that would need to be true in order for you to have your outcome. You can also phrase the question in the past tense: *What would need to have happened if this outcome were true?*

If you don't know where to begin, start with who, what, where, when, why, and how. That's what we're going for.

Example: What would need to have happened if I opened a flower shop?

1. *Make sure shop is in great location.*

2. *Get a business license.*

3. *Purchase inventory from flower wholesaler.*

Your turn. What needs to be true in order for your dream vision to be realized?

1. _____

2. _____

3. _____

4. _____

5. _____

6. _____

Now look at the six individual items on your list. Write these items in the numbered spaces below. Alongside the bullets in the space provided, write out the steps you need to take to achieve each of these items. These are your action points, the things that you will do to make your six items happen.

Examples: Research shops for rent or sale in high traffic areas. Look for a place with a great storefront and room in the back for working on flower arrangements. Find out what licenses will be needed to run a business. Apply for any licenses or certifications that will help legitimize the business. Research wholesale prices for flowers. Find a wholesaler or retailer with good prices and quick and reliable delivery to my area.

1. _____

   • _____

   • _____

   • _____

2. _____

   • _____

- _____
- _____

3. _____

- _____
- _____
- _____

4. _____

- _____
- _____
- _____

5. _____

- _____
- _____
- _____

6. _____

- _____
- _____
- _____

KEEP MOVING FORWARD

When you complete the one-page action plan exercise, you will have a workable plan for how to bring your vision to life and make your outcome a reality. If, like Maura's, your dream is a big one and requires a lot of thought and action, consider breaking each of the steps out into a new worksheet, so that each step is its own vision with its own list of six items and its own action points. With large goals action plans give birth to new action plans, and each iteration will bring you closer to achieving your dreams.

As you learned in Chapter 3, when you create, and then complete or check off an item on a written list, your brain generates a happiness hit of dopamine. It gives new meaning to the sense of accomplishment you have when you're on a mission: there is a real euphoria connected to meeting goals, and there is no greater high than being high on life. You can get those tiny happiness hits anytime or anywhere, even when you trip and fall into a metaphorical hole. Even writing down *Create my daily to-do list* and then checking it off (since you just did it) is like giving your brain a big hug. (You can get a tiny dopamine hit by checking off anything else from your Zen 10 too.)

When I fell into that personal abyss that I talked about in Chapter 6, it became a huge turning point for me to use this tool of the one-page action plan to help me heal. I believe it will be a turning point for you too. When I was in that dark place, I felt self-conscious about even admitting that I felt depressed. As I mentioned I tried all my other reliable pick-me-up methods—exercise, affirmations, watching funny movies—but nothing lifted the fog. At that point not only was I depressed and foggy, but I was also in confusion and negative self-evaluation: *What was so wrong that I wasn't feeling unwavering joy all the time, especially since I saw myself as a person who helps solve life's complications?* I had never seen myself as someone who got caught up in life's worries, but there I was—feeling pinned down and trapped by an unidentifiable weight.

When I decided to take a step back and assess the situation, I asked myself, *What's wrong here?* This is when I made that list, the list of everything that was wrong in my life. Right away I felt relief. It helped me realize that I had enough big things happening in my life that I would be crazy if I *weren't* affected by all of them. That part of my process is what I call "reaching in and shining the flashlight into the corner." If you want to see where you can take some action, and since you know that having a plan will make you feel better, reach into the hole and switch on the flashlight.

If you're feeling stumped at the moment, reread Chapter 6 and revisit whatever it was you said you needed to solve. Remember that at any time you can write your action plan about your desires, any problems you have, or any long-term solution you need to find. Whatever you're facing, writing out a plan will help.

Then take one step, one slight move in that general direction toward *What needs to happen for me to reach my goal/resolve this issue?* Get it out of your head, onto paper, and get it checked off of your list. When you get things out of your mind, you don't have to track them anymore. This alone will improve your chemical recipe, and it will also raise your position on the frequency scale. And then move on to the next item.

Making a one-page action plan is the *how* answer to that overwhelming *what* question. And if you act on it, it will take you from chaos to clarity.

MY HOPE

If I could distill this book into one piece of advice, it would be this: Get all the areas of your life in alignment with your dreams. All of them. Get every choice and action in alignment. With the right choices, the right thoughts, the right words, you can develop pathways to steer your life toward your deepest desires.

Those actions, choices, words, and thoughts create your reality every day. If your desire is to lose weight, you have to get every action, choice, word, and thought in alignment with that desire so that it can become reality. That means going to the gym, taking your vitamins, getting a physical. But it also means, through your words and actions, telling yourself—and others—truths that support that goal, not the same negative thoughts that keep you reaching for that pint of ice cream at the end of every day.

Whatever you desire, say *no* to everything that moves you farther away from that goal, and say *yes* only to things that move you closer to it.

By now you're probably feeling a mixture of hope, excitement, and anxiety. I know that feeling. Just think: you can finally make that plan, take on the smaller tasks, design your ideal life, and get traction on taking action. How does it feel to be on the verge of the life you always imagined? If I were to tell my 5- or 10-years-younger self one thing, it would be the same thing I'm telling you, which is that you really can have anything you want. It can be yours the minute your actions line up with your desires. Don't let fear block the actions you know you need to take; stop holding yourself back. Eliminate the word *try* from your vocabulary and replace it with *will*. An easy filter for whether you'll take action on your dreams is to ask yourself, *What is the cost of not taking action?*

I have an answer to that, and there's no easy way to say it: There *is* a cost of not taking action toward your dreams. Imagine living the rest of your life with regret, bitter and dissatisfied because your life wasn't what you wanted it to be—and knowing that you have no one to blame but yourself.

Know this: you are only as powerful as the action you're willing to take. Put your dreams in charge, not your fears, and understand that it takes courage to do anything worth doing, including making a change in the landscape of your life.

Submit to the greatness within, and let that greatness tell you where to go and what to do next. Take action like your life depends on it, because it does. What is your Greatness Potential? How can you find your drive, your willingness to do things differently than everyone else, to find your own way? How can you be a shining example of what humanity can be?

That's a lot of pressure, I know. So one last thing: don't worry about getting it "exactly right." If you try and you get it "wrong," even a hundred times, it just means you will be that much better every time you try after that. So instead of comparing yourself to anyone else, look within. Take action in the ways that make your life a unique expression of your most authentic self.

Now is the time to bring your thoughts, words, choices, and actions into alignment with what you desire and who you really are.

Now that you know how to make your dreams come true, what will you dream?

Now that you know where your power is, how will your life be different?

Right *now*, how can you take action?

ACKNOWLEDGMENTS

I'd like to send a big thank you to my family, especially my boys Keagan and Hayden. As your Mom, I strive daily to teach you, though I think I end up learning from you so much more! Gratitude to my friends who had a particularly special role, whether as support, giving advice, or listening: Andrew Timms, Guy Kufahl, Jeff and Kristen Geis, Brett Hays, and Renee Angelah. Also to those many friends I have made, by purpose or fate, along my many adventures—we have broken bread, roomed together, powered through hours of travel, and shared new roads on this awesome journey—I cherish you all but I especially need to thank Will Harris, Miachel Hancock-Eccles, Nahla Abbo, and last but not least Lee Milteer!

A very special thank you to my daily gratitude group: Bianca Hearfield, Sara Yupcavage, and Lisa Peers. I know, without a shadow of a doubt, that the first step to manifesting this book was creating our gratitude group. I am so fortunate that the choices we made brought us together.

To my amazing staff who have made it possible for me to focus on writing and developing this book. I value and appreciate each and every one of you! Marie, Roxie, Deb, Alex, Trish, John, and Roxanne—my Platform Team. You helped me to springboard into a whole new world! I couldn't have done this without you!

To my teachers, including, but not limited to Louise Hay, Mike Dooley, and Tony Robbins: I am ever so grateful because, more than you know, you have helped me heal, grow, and achieve my dreams!

To my dream publisher Hay House Publishing and Sally Mason, KN Literary Arts (Lizzie Vance, Kelly Notaras, and Nikki

Van De Car), and Thunderstruck Designs. You are the professionals without whom I'd be lost. A huge thank you for your expertise and artistry!

I'd also like to thank my writer's group at Omega Institute, the Monroe Institute, and Parkland College. Special thanks to Ebertfest and Chaz Ebert (You are a powerhouse, continuing to keep Roger's legacy alive!) for providing the opportunity for me to encounter Chazz Palminteri. C, thank you for your confidence and guidance.

And . . . thank YOU! Thank you for reading, dreaming, and being fearlessly ambitious!

ABOUT THE AUTHOR

Mary Shores is the owner and founder of one of the most unique collection agencies in the country, which focuses on positive communication, integrity, and accountability. Recognized as a leader of innovative thought, she has spent over a decade teaching businesses and individuals how to inspire others, create new ways of thinking, identify their goals, and take action to create meaningful results. She is the innovative founder of the groundbreaking Conscious Communications system. Mary travels across the nation giving lectures and teaching courses and has been featured on local and national radio and television shows, podcasts, and blogs. To learn more, visit MaryShores.com.

We hope you enjoyed this Hay House book.
If you'd like to receive our online catalog featuring additional information
on Hay House books and products, or if you'd like to find out more about
the Hay Foundation, please contact:

Hay House, Inc.
P.O. Box 5100
Carlsbad, CA 92018-5100

(760) 431-7695 or **(800) 654-5126**
(760) 431-6948 (fax) or **(800) 650-5115 (fax)**
www.hayhouse.com® • **www.hayfoundation.org**

Published and distributed in Australia by: Hay House Australia Pty. Ltd.,
18/36 Ralph St., Alexandria NSW 2015 • *Phone:* 612-9669-4299
Fax: 612-9669-4144 www.hayhouse.com.au

Published and distributed in the United Kingdom by: Hay House UK, Ltd.,
Astley House, 33 Notting Hill Gate, London W11 3JQ
Phone: 44-20-3675-2450 • *Fax:* 44-20-3675-2451
www.hayhouse.co.uk

Published and distributed in the Republic of South Africa by:
Hay House SA (Pty), Ltd., P.O. Box 990, Witkoppen 2068
info@hayhouse.co.za • www.hayhouse.co.za

Published in India by: Hay House Publishers India, Muskaan Complex,
Plot No. 3, B-2, Vasant Kunj, New Delhi 110 070 • *Phone:* 91-11-4176-1620
Fax: 91-11-4176-1630 • www.hayhouse.co.in

Distributed in Canada by: Raincoast Books, 2440 Viking Way,
Richmond, B.C. V6V 1N2 • *Phone:* 1-800-663-5714
Fax: 1-800-565-3770 • www.raincoast.com

***

Access New Knowledge.
Anytime. Anywhere.

Learn and evolve at your own pace with the world's leading experts.

www.hayhouseU.com